Children, Families, and
Health Care Decision Making

LAINIE FRIEDMAN ROSS

CLARENDON PRESS · OXFORD

*This book has been printed digitally and produced in a standard specification
in order to ensure its continuing availability*

OXFORD
UNIVERSITY PRESS

Great Clarendon Street, Oxford OX2 6DP

Oxford University Press is a department of the University of Oxford.
It furthers the University's objective of excellence in research, scholarship,
and education by publishing worldwide in

Oxford New York

Auckland Cape Town Dar es Salaam Hong Kong Karachi
Kuala Lumpur Madrid Melbourne Mexico City Nairobi
New Delhi Shanghai Taipei Toronto
With offices in
Argentina Austria Brazil Chile Czech Republic France Greece
Guatemala Hungary Italy Japan South Korea Poland Portugal
Singapore Switzerland Thailand Turkey Ukraine Vietnam

Oxford is a registered trade mark of Oxford University Press
in the UK and in certain other countries

Published in the United States
by Oxford University Press Inc., New York

ISBN 0-19-925154-1

Antony Rowe Ltd., Eastbourne

ISSUES IN BIOMEDICAL ETHICS

*Children, Families, and Health Care
Decision Making*

ISSUES IN BIOMEDICAL ETHICS

General Editors
John Harris and Søren Holm

Consulting Editors
Ranaan Gillon and Bonnie Steinbock

The late twentieth century has witnessed dramatic technological developments in biomedical science and the delivery of health care, and these developments have brought with them important social changes. All too often ethical analysis has lagged behind these changes. The purpose of this series is to provide lively, up-to-date, and authoritative studies for the increasingly large and diverse readership concerned with issues in biomedical ethics— not just healthcare trainees and professionals, but also philosophers, social scientists, lawyers, social workers, and legislators. The series will feature both single-author and multi-author books, short and accessible enough to be widely read, each of them focused on an issue of outstanding current importance and interest. Philosophers, doctors, and lawyers from a number of countries feature among the authors lined up for the series.

I dedicate this book to my parents, Eleanor and Arthur Friedman, who knew how to promote my autonomy without abandoning me to it.

A doctor has opportunities for studying human nature which are given to no one else, wherefore a philosopher ought to begin his life as a doctor, and a doctor should end his life by becoming a philosopher.

—*Ancient Greek saying*

Acknowledgements

This book is the culmination of a challenging journey that began in my senior year at Princeton, when I stumbled into two political philosophy classes. I decided then to combine medicine with moral and political philosophy. My knowledge of medical ethics was limited to my brief exposure to Paul Ramsey, who taught a course entitled 'Christian Ethics'. I planned to read philosophy, particularly medical ethics, during the seven years of medical school and paediatric training. Few will be surprised to learn that my reading was sparse.

I began my philosophy studies at Yale University in 1989. I had applied while I was still finishing my paediatric residency and needed letters of recommendation. Dr Steve Ludwig at the Children's Hospital of Philadelphia and Dr Jennifer Bell at Babies' Hospital of Columbia University in New York City were wonderful. Neither had written a letter of recommendation to a philosophy department before. I'm still not sure whether it's important for my philosophical studies that I remain calm during a medical emergency, but their belief in my capabilities convinced the admissions committee at Yale.

At Yale, I met a diverse group of colleagues. Sarah Broadie, Walter Glannon, and Dave Schmidtz of the Philosophy Department were integral to my intellectual transformation. I owe an equally deep-felt thank-you to my non-philosophy colleagues who made my education complete: Margaret Farley and Richard Fern in the Yale Divinity School and Jay Katz at Yale Law School.

My Yale experience would not have been complete without my husband, John Ross, whom I married two weeks before I matriculated. He was the only person who understood from the beginning why I wanted to pursue this path. His support was unwavering. He also encouraged me to take time off from paediatrics in order to immerse myself in my new endeavour. My paediatric sabbatical lasted nine months by which time I missed the children too much. I thank Ron Blumenfeld at the Community Health Care Plan (CHCP) in Bridgeport, Connecticut, for offering me a job which allowed me the flexible hours required of a student whose schedule changes every semester. And a warm hug to Varsha Shah, who was the colleague who kept rearranging her own schedule to accommodate mine.

I left Yale in 1994 for the University of Chicago, with appointments in the Department of Paediatrics and the MacLean Center for Clinical Medical Ethics. Colleagues in both the Department and the Center have been supportive of my career path. I owe deep gratitude to Mary Mahowald, who encouraged me to finish my dissertation when no one else, myself included, seemed to care. I also greatly appreciate the advice and support of the Center's director, Mark Siegler, and the many conversations I have enjoyed with colleagues, despite our procedural and substantive disagreements.

This book is based on my Ph.D. dissertation, 'Health Care Decision Making for Children'. A special thanks to Robin Downie, whose work inspired my research. I sent him a copy of the finished dissertation because I believed it represented an extension of his project of applying the principle of respect for persons to health care. He encouraged me to revise my dissertation into this book, and to submit the manuscript to Oxford University Press. I thank all of the editors with whom I worked for their help in getting the manuscript into its present form.

I owe an extra thanks to those individuals who read earlier versions of the manuscript in its entirety: Robin Downie, Richard Fern, Shelly Kagan, Jay Katz, John Lantos, Mary Mahowald, Robert Merrill, Tom Roby, and Dave Schmidtz. Walter Glannon and John Ross read and re-read many chapters at many different stages and their patience is appreciated.

I owe two special thank-yous. First, a special thank-you to Stan and Ann Dudley Goldblatt for their unwavering support on the value of this project. Second, a special thank-you to John Ross, who kept updating my computer hardware and software so that each version presented technical advances that I am yet to appreciate fully.

Several of the chapters draw heavily on previously published articles. I wish to thank the relevant editors and publishers for permission to use material from the following:

'Moral Grounding for the Participation of Children as Organ

Donors', *Journal of Law, Medicine, and Ethics*, 21 (2) (Summer 1993), 251–7.

'Justice for Children: The Child as Organ Donor', *Bioethics*, 8 (2) (April 1994), 105–26.

'Arguments Against Health Care Autonomy for Minors', *Bioethics Forum*, 11 (4) (Winter 1995), 22–6.

'Adolescent Sexuality and Public Policy: A Liberal Response', *Politics and the Life Sciences*, 15 (1), (March 1996), 13–21.

'Adolescent Sexuality and Public Policy: An Unrepentant Liberal Approach', *Politics and the Life Sciences*, 15 (2) (September 1996), 323–8.

'Children as Research Subjects: A Proposal to Revise the Federal Regulations Using a Moral Framework', *Stanford Law and Policy Review*, 8 (1) (Winter 1997), 159–76.

'Health Care Autonomy for Minors: Is It in Their Best Interest?', *Hastings Center Report*, 27 (6) (November–December 1997), 41–5.

I would also like to thank the *New England Journal of Medicine* and the Massachusetts Medical Society for allowing me to reprint the case of Baby L. The full article is published as J. J. Paris, R. K. Crone, and F. Reardon, 'Occasional Notes: Physicians' Refusal of Requested Treatment—The Case of Baby L', *New England Journal of Medicine*, 322 (5 April 1990), 1012–15.

Finally, I owe everlasting gratitude to my wonderful family. I am truly fortunate to have been reared in an intact, intimate family. The additions of nieces and nephews, my brothers' spouses, my daughters, my husband, and his family have further convinced me that an ethics of the family is critical for an understanding of the obligations that are created voluntarily and involuntarily within this primary institution.

Contents

PART I

The Development of a Health Care Decision-Making Model for Children

1

Introduction

1. *Children, Families, and Decision Making*

My purpose in writing this book is to examine how decisions should be made for children, with a focus primarily on health care decisions. I argue that in a liberal society, decisions about a child's health care should be made by his or her parents. In order for parents to make health care decisions for their child, they must balance the child's health needs, his or her needs for other primary goods, and the needs and interests of other family members. To make these decisions in a way that reflects their values and beliefs, parents need wide latitude. I reject the present 'best interest of the child' standard in favour of a standard that allows parents more flexibility. I propose a standard that is based on the principle of respect for persons modified to accommodate the child's developing personhood.

In the first half of this book, I propose a decision-making model for children that emphasizes parental autonomy constrained by respect for the child's developing personhood. I call this model 'constrained parental autonomy'. In the second half, I show how this model works in various health care settings.

2. *Background: The Child, the Family, and the Liberal State*

Liberalism is a political theory of limited government which provides institutional guarantees of personal liberties and basic rights for its adult members. Adults are free to devise and implement their own life plans. This includes the freedom to form and raise a family according to their own conception of the good. Less clear-cut is how liberalism deals with children.

Scant attention has been paid to the family and its children members by liberal theorists during the last quarter of the century. Jeffrey Blustein hypothesized in 1982 that contemporary moral theorists ignore children and the family 'because they tend to conceive of ethics as the study of those principles that determine how *any* two individuals are required to regard, and behave toward, one another'.[1] Contemporary theorists emphasize impartiality and universalizability, and either dismiss the interactions within the family as an exception to these ethical concepts or subsume family relationships as special relationships which entail particular obligations. Although there has been a recent emergence of writings of partialistic ethics and ethics of personal relationships, these works focus on adult friendship and marriage and less on children and families.[2]

The history of the philosophy of the family shows that this has not always been the case. From Plato to Russell, all liberal theorists discussed the family and the importance of the family in the moral development of individuals.[3] In contrast, contemporary liberal theorists generally assume, as did Hobbes, that the moral agents of liberal theory are 'as if but now sprung out of the earth . . . like mushrooms'.[4]

My purpose is not to offer a theory of a child's moral development, a task best left to the moral psychologists, whose work I rely upon in discussing the concept of child competency and its relationship to child autonomy (Chapter 4). Rather, my purpose is to examine how decisions ought to be made for children in a liberal society which depends upon an understanding of the moral development of children and the moral function of the family. Although some contemporary liberal theorists have recommended empowering children with rights and allowing them to make decisions for themselves,[5] classical liberal theorists did not.[6] I will argue, too, against empowering children with rights because such a strategy fails on at least three levels. First, it fails to recognize the child's need to gain the skills and virtues necessary to make decisions that promote the child's lifetime well-being. Second, it fails to recognize the parents' role in helping to define the child's well-being and conception of the good. Third, it fails to respect the parents' interest in child-rearing.

My understanding of the proper role of parents and children in a liberal society incorporates several assumptions. First, I assume that children are members of intimate families. I realize that there are children who are not members of families (e.g. orphans) and that some children are members of families that are not intimate. Whether my proposal can be modified to accommodate such children or whether another decision-making model is necessary is a future project.

What does it mean to be a member of a family, particularly a member of an intimate family? There is no simple definition of the family, and in fact, it is more accurate to talk about families.[7] Families take many shapes, have variable size, and differ as to whom is included as a member. The definitions of families vary in time and among cultures. For example, in early tribal communities, extended families were the norm, whereas today most households are nuclear. Today, homosexual couples are recognized as families in some cities and not in others. While the legal definition of family is based on biology and contract, many heterosexual couples as well as lesbian and gay couples live in de facto marriages without state sanction, and over one-quarter of children born in the United States today are not born to legally married parents.[8] What counts as family is further complicated by the high rates of divorce and remarriage, as well as the new reproductive technologies and their ability to separate genetic from gestational motherhood and genetic from social parenthood.

My focus is on families with non-emancipated children (children who are below the legal age of majority). As such, I use the term 'family' to signify a relationship of two or more individuals in which at least one is an adult who is capable of and responsible for providing for the 'primary goods' of at least one child.[9] Such a family is intimate if there is significant interdependence among the members and a commitment to the well-being of each other and the group. This definition is too broad in that it applies to some groups of adults and children who are not generally viewed as families (e.g. religious communities). What distinguishes an intimate family with non-emancipated children from other intimate groups is the obligation to procure (or make provisions for the procurement of) *all* of the child's primary goods. Parent(s) in an intimate family must provide (or make provisions for the fulfilment of) *all* of their child's 'basic needs',[10] which include the basic goods, skills, and liberties, and opportunities essential for the adequate development and full exercise of moral personality.[11]

Parents are not purely altruistic and self-sacrificing, nor is their sole function the provision of their child's primary goods. For many adults, rearing a child in an environment in which their values and beliefs flourish is a principal reason for becoming parents. In a liberal society, parents are free to inculcate their children with their own values. They are free to shape and guide their child's future lifestyle and life plans. Of course, parents are not totally free: for example, parents cannot deprive their daughters of a primary education, although they are free to select the type of school that their daughters attend. As such, parents have great influence on the values to which their children are exposed, even in institutions outside of the family. As a result, most individuals hold values and beliefs that are strongly influenced by their parents. Although parents have no guarantee that their child will accept their values and beliefs, it takes great motivation and self-reflection to do otherwise.

My conception of an intimate family is an intimate group in which the parent–child relationship and its attendant obligations are central. This conception includes some legal families and excludes others. It also includes many non-traditional, non-legally sanctioned families. The intimate family is a moral and not a biological or legally defined relationship.[12]

A complete theory of the family must address all the different relationships within the family. It needs to address the responsibilities and obligations of the mature adults to each other, to their children, to their elderly parents, and to their extended families as well as the relationships and obligations of young children to their siblings, parents, and extended relations. Such a theory must address, for example, whether we have special obligations to estranged partners, former in-laws, or to cousins we have never met. I offer only a limited theory of the family, focusing on the non-emancipated child and his relationships with his parents, although I touch upon the child's relationships to his siblings.

Second, I assume that the child's biological parents have and should have primary child-rearing responsibility. Arguments have been made to assign child-rearing on other criteria, including capability, lottery, justice, or to assign to the state primary child-rearing responsibility.[13] And in some communities, individuals other than biological parents do have primary child-rearing responsibilities.[14] Nevertheless, in modern liberal societies, biological parents are the presumptive social parents, no matter from where this authority is derived.[15] Any attempt to reassign children to adults other than their biological parents will require no less than a radical upheaval of present-day society, a radical transition for which there is little popular demand. However, some children are not reared by their biological parents. The authority and responsibility of biological parents are defeasible both voluntarily (e.g. when biological parents give their child up for adoption) and involuntarily (e.g. when the state takes control of abused children).

Third, I assume that the family is an important institution in the lives of most people and that even if child-rearing could take place outside of the family, where it might be performed more equitably and efficiently, most individuals would be loath to forfeit this opportunity. Many adults seem to choose to bear and rear children as part of their vision of the good life.

Fourth, I assume in the first three chapters that all children are incompetent to make health care decisions and that they should not have presumptive decision-making autonomy. Most theories about decision making in health care assume an adult patient who is presumed to be competent. These theories maintain that the patient's autonomy ought to be respected unless the patient can be shown to be incompetent. The assumptions that children are incompetent and that their autonomy should not be respected may not be problematic for most readers, particularly when the child is young. These assumptions need to be justified in the older more rational child who may possess a threshold level of competency. In Chapter 4, I review the empirical data regarding the competency of older children to make health care decisions. Although some children have attained a threshold level of competency, I argue that competency is a necessary but not a sufficient condition to justify respect for the child's autonomy. Nevertheless, children, particularly those who have attained a threshold level of competency, should not be ignored in the decision-making process even if they should not have decision-making autonomy. The model of constrained parental autonomy supports a role for children which depends on the child's degree of competency, the type of decision, and the context in which the decision is being made.

3. *Book Outline: Part I*

The model of constrained parental autonomy assumes that parents and children are members of intimate families in a liberal society in which parents have primary responsibility for providing for their children's basic needs. The quantity and type of a particular primary good are mainly defined by parents who will give their children varying amounts of each good depending on their conception of the good life. Different parents will distribute different goods in different quantities and different forms depending upon their beliefs and values. In liberal communities, the state tolerates a wide range of distributions among families provided that the parents provide their children with a threshold level of each primary good. Parents require wide latitude to balance the health care needs of their child with the child's need for other primary goods, and with the needs of other family members.

A family-oriented approach to decision making for children should begin with a theory of the family, or at minimum, with a theory of how families should make decisions, what principles should guide them, and what ought to be the limits of family autonomy. In Chapter 2, I offer a critical examination of two contemporary theories of the family. I have chosen the works of Jeffrey Blustein and Laurence Houlgate as they illustrate, respectively, a deontological and utilitarian approach to a theory of the family. Despite their conceptual differences, they have two problems which are common in modern theories of the family. First, both theories deal almost exclusively with issues of distributions and decisions between families and do not address intrafamilial distributions and decisions. The family is assumed to be an entity whose members have compatible goals and interests. Although many goals of intimates are interwoven and interdependent, I believe that a theory of the family must also allow for the expression of individual identity and the pursuit of individual goals by each member, including its children members.

A second problem common to both theories is the assumption that the family exists solely to serve the children. These theories ignore the fact that 'the family is not self-conceived as primarily an institution or community existing to benefit children'.[16] Parents bear and rear children for selfish as well as selfless reasons, and for self-regarding as well as other-regarding interests. Theories that focus sole attention on the child-rearing functions of families ignore the importance that adults ascribe to the creation of a home in which their values flourish. Although my focus is on families with non-emancipated children, an adequate theory must incorporate the needs and interests of the parents. I offer a (partial) theory of the family which respects the role that the intimate family plays in the lives of *all* its members.

Despite these problems, Blustein and Houlgate highlight some of the important characteristics which I believe that a theory of the family must include. In particular, Houlgate's communal model of the family is based on the characteristics of a *Gemeinschaft* (community) in contrast to a *Gesellschaft* (organization).[17] Why this strict dichotomy fails helps clarify the essential features of an intimate family.

In general, parents are assumed to be the appropriate decision makers for their children. The focus of Chapter 3 is to determine what principles should guide parental decision making with regard to their children. Presently, the two principles used to guide surrogate decision makers are the principles of substituted judgement and the best interest standard. Substituted judgement is a principle which requires a surrogate decision maker to act as the patient would act if he or she were competent. If the individual's beliefs are specifically known (e.g. through an advance directive), then the surrogate is supposed to follow these directions; otherwise the surrogate is supposed to 'don the mantle of the incompetent'[18] in order that the decision reflect and respect the patient's individuality and dignity. The principle is designed to accommodate the subjective beliefs and values of the particular patient. *Ideally* it would be employed *only* for formerly competent individuals whose preferences are known or can be inferred from other known values.[19]

Under the best interest standard, the surrogate is not guided by the patient's wishes but weighs all relevant factors and decides what is in the patient's best interest, all things considered. This standard is appropriate when the patient has no known or competently expressed preferences. When the patient is a child, this standard is more appropriate than the substituted judgement standard because a surrogate cannot act as the child would act if competent, when the child has not yet achieved competency.

Under the best interest standard, parents are usually presumed to be in the best position to decide what is in their child's best interest, and they often go to great lengths to promote their child's interests. There are many problems, however, with holding parents to a best interest standard. For example, it would require parents to sacrifice any of their short-term or long-term goals for their child because it would require that a parent disregard all personal interests in order to fulfil the child's needs, interests, and wants. That parents are individuals with interests, needs, and rights is ignored. The standard also leaves no room for compromise, and does not offer a viable solution for dealing with a family in which there is more than one child, each with competing and conflicting best interest claims. Parents need wide latitude in defining their child's needs and how they should be procured, and an appropriate guidance principle for parental decisions must permit wide parental autonomy. I propose that parental autonomy should be constrained by a modified principle of respect for persons.

The principle of respect for persons formulated by Kant states: 'Act in such a way that you treat humanity, whether in your own person or in the person of another, always at the same time as an end and never simply as a means.'[20] Some argue that Kant's principle of respect for persons applies only to fully rational beings; others argue that it applies to persons and potential persons.[21] There is also disagreement whether the principle refers to respect for the rights of persons, or respect for the potentials of persons.[22] Similarly there is no agreement whether respect for persons is a moral principle like truth-telling, or whether it is *the* fundamental moral principle by which all other moral principles can be explained.[23]

It is not my purpose to resolve these debates. Rather, I assume that the principle of respect for persons is a fundamental moral principle, and that respect is owed not only to Kantian persons, but to developing persons.[24] Children, particularly young children, are not Kantian persons, but they are developing persons and they deserve respect.[25] However, children do not deserve the same respect due to the mature rational adult (i.e. Kantian person) but they deserve respect because of their potential to become persons and to the extent that they have actualized some of the characteristics associated with personhood.[26]

Because children are not Kantian persons, the Kantian principle of respect for persons does not apply to them. Instead, children are developing persons and a principle of respect that applies to them is needed.[27] A principle of respect that applies to children must account for their potential to become Kantian persons and the degree to which they have already actualized some of the characteristics associated with personhood. A twelve-month-old and a twelve-year-old both have the potential to become Kantian persons, but the twelve-year-old has already actualized more of the characteristics that we associate with personhood; namely, the ability to articulate goals and to rationally deliberate between some choices. If respect is owed proportionate to one's actualization of the characteristics of personhood, then the older child is deserving of greater respect.

In Chapter 3, I explore what is meant by a principle of respect modified to apply to children. I begin by modifying Kant's second formulation of the categorical imperative to apply to children: 'Children should never be treated *solely* as a means, but always, at the same time, as developing persons and as individuals who have actualized some of the characteristics associated with personhood.' I understand this to include two overlapping components:

1. a negative component which applies universally and which prohibits the abuse, neglect, and exploitation of children; and

2. a positive component which applies only in particular relationships and which incorporates the duty to provide children with the primary goods necessary to become persons capable of devising and implementing their own life plans.

Both components vary depending on the relationship of the child and the individual from whom respect is due. Whereas neither a parent nor a stranger should treat the child *solely* as a means, only the parent needs to give the child the skills or goods that will help the child flourish. While a stranger has only the obligation not to harm the child, parents have an obligation to help promote the child's potential. This does not mean that a child has a claim against his parents or other intimates to be exposed to the widest range of possible ways of life. Nor does it mean that the child has a claim against his peers to compensate for those skills and goods which his parents choose not to offer him. The principle requires only that parents and other intimates provide the child with the means and skills necessary to achieve a viable life plan. Whether parents offer their child a wide array of lifestyles or a narrow, ascetic lifestyle is their prerogative.

The principle of respect for persons, modified to apply to children, is the principle that I propose to guide parents in their decision making for their children's health care. This guidance principle allows parents wide discretion in defining and balancing their child's health care needs against the child's other needs and interests as well as against the needs and interests of other family members.

In Chapter 4, I consider what function the child's competency ought to play in the decision-making process. I argue that competency is a necessary but not a sufficient condition to require respect for a child's autonomy, and that parental authority is appropriate, even when children are competent. Granting autonomy to competent children too early may be autonomy-restricting over a lifetime because it abandons the child to his own decision making without providing a protected period in which he can develop the capacities needed to flourish. This is not to deny that the child's growing competency should have some bearing on his role in the decision-making process. Parents have an increasing moral obligation to consider the expressed beliefs and wishes of their child as the child matures, and there may even be some cases in which respect for the child's developing and partially actualized personhood requires that the child's assent or dissent be binding. I consider such cases in Part II.

4. *Part II: Application of the Model*

In the second half of the book, I illustrate how the model of constrained parental autonomy works in a variety of health care settings. My goals are (1) to show how the model of constrained parental autonomy, unlike a model based on the best interest standard, can permit families to pursue goals even when they compromise the best interests of their children; and (2) to explore the limits to parental autonomy in health care decisions. I show that parental decisions regarding health care are valid only within a certain range, and that there are some decisions which are not acceptable, even when parents and children consent to them.

In Chapter 5, I examine the role of the child as a subject in human experimentation. The National Commission for the Protection of Human Subjects distinguished between four types of research: research that entails minimal risk, research that entails a minor increase over minimal risk, research that entails more than a minor increase over minimal risk, and research that offers the prospect of direct therapeutic benefit. It also distinguished between two classes of children: children able to give assent and those who are not. From this starting block, I revise and expand the classification of research into five categories (adding research that offers the prospect of indirect therapeutic benefit and entails no more than a minor increase over minimal risk). I reclassify children into three categories by subdividing the class of children who can give assent into those who are competent and can give consent versus those who are incompetent and can give only assent.[28] I use this revised classification scheme to explore the limits of parental autonomy and the proper role of children in the research setting. I conclude that the dissent of children ought to be binding in fewer cases than it presently is, and that some research that is presently permitted should be prohibited, whether or not the parents and the children agree to participate.

In Chapter 6, I discuss the participation of a child as an organ donor for a sibling. To participate as an organ donor is to participate in health care which is not done for one's own benefit, although the donor may gain some indirect benefit from her participation. I distinguish between donations of minimal and a minor increase over minimal risk and donations that entail more than a minor increase over minimal risk. I argue that parental autonomy alone is sufficient for donations that do not entail more than a minor increase over minimal risk, but that parents should not be allowed to make unilateral decisions when there is greater than a minor increase over minimal risk. Rather, for donations that entail more than a minor increase over minimal risk, the consent of the competent child and his parents are necessary, and the participation of incompetent children is impermissible whether or not the child and his parents assent to the procedure.

In Chapter 7, I discuss therapeutic (non-experimental) health care. The main focus of this chapter is to explore two sets of cases that challenge the limits of parental autonomy. The first kind involves parental refusals of standard medical care. Refusals may be based on religious belief (e.g. the Jehovah's Witness who refuses to authorize a blood transfusion for her child), holistic beliefs (e.g. the parent who believes in megavitamins rather than chemotherapeutic 'poisons' for the treatment of cancer), or misunderstanding (e.g. the parents who do not complete their child's course of antibiotics because the child is feeling better). When the treatment is non-experimental and very effective, parental refusals risk their child's medical well-being and are contrary to the principle of respect as it applies to children. However, the state should limit its interventions to those cases in which (1) the illness is life-threatening or places the child at high risk for serious and significant morbidity, and (2) the treatment is of proven efficacy with a high probability of success.

The second kind involves cases where parents seek treatment over the objection of the providing physicians who argue that the treatment is futile and inhumane. I argue that most cases of futility are quality-of-life judgements, which properly belong to the patient and his or her surrogates. However, there may be a point when the treatment is both 'virtually futile and inhumane', and parents could be prohibited from authorizing such care.[29]

Chapter 8 looks at the issue of sexual and reproductive health care for adolescents. Presently there are specialized consent statutes in all fifty U.S. states which empower adolescents to procure confidential care for specific medical conditions. I argue that these statutes inappropriately exclude the majority of parents who are able and willing to make these decisions with and on behalf of their children.

Chapters 5 through 8 are meant to illustrate the wide range of health care topics which a decision-making model for children must address. Constrained parental autonomy as applied to health care issues respects wide latitude in parental and family autonomy while it simultaneously ensures that the decisions give children the respect they are due.

One caveat. Constrained parental autonomy is a model about

decision making for children in intimate families, not an algorithm. Its application requires interpretation in light of particular circumstances. There may be some cases where the reader disagrees with my conclusions. If one accepts the arguments in the first half of this book, these differences should be the exception rather than the rule and should not detract from my overall purpose.

Notes

1. J. Blustein, *Parents and Children: The Ethics of the Family* (New York: Oxford University Press, 1982), 19.
2. See, for example, N. K. Badhwar (ed.), *Friendship: A Philosophical Reader* (New York: Cornell University Press, 1993); M. Friedman, *What Are Friends For?* (New York: Cornell University Press, 1993); G. Graham and H. LaFollette (eds.), *Person to Person* (Philadelphia, Pa.: Temple University Press, 1989); and H. LaFollette, *Personal Relationships: Love, Identity, and Morality* (Cambridge, Mass.: Blackwell Publishers, 1996). One recent anthology that deals with children and parents is edited by G. Scarre, *Children, Parents, and Politics* (New York: Cambridge University Press, 1989).
3. Blustein, *Parents and Children*, Part I, 17–98.
4. T. Hobbes, 'Philosophical Rudiments Concerning Government and Society', in W. Molesworth (ed.), *The English Works of Thomas Hobbes*, ii (London: John Bohn, 1966), 109.
5. See, for example, H. Cohen, *Equal Rights for Children* (Totowa, NJ: Littlefield, Adams, 1980); J. Holt, *Escape from Childhood* (New York: E. P. Dutton, 1974); and H. Rodham, 'Children Under the Law', *Harvard Educational Review*, 43 (1973), 487–514.
6. J. Locke, *Two Treatises of Government* (1690), ed. P. Laslett (New York: Cambridge University Press, 1963).
7. S. M. Dornbusch and M. H. Strober, 'Our Perspective', in S. M. Dornbusch and M. H. Strober (eds.), *Feminism, Children, and the New Families* (New York: Guildford Press, 1988), 3–24. See also B. Thorne, 'Feminism and the Family: Two Decades of Thought', in B. Thorne with M. Yalom (eds.), *Rethinking the Family: Some Feminist Questions*, rev. ed. (Boston, Mass.: Northeastern University Press, 1992), 3–30.
8. National Center for Health Statistics, 'Advance Report of Final Natality Statistics, 1990', *Monthly Vital Statistics Report*, 41 Supp. (1993), 33, table 16.
9. Rawls, in *A Theory of Justice*, defines 'primary goods' as 'things which

it is supposed a rational man wants, whatever else he wants'. J. Rawls, *A Theory of Justice* (Cambridge, Mass.: Belknap Press of Harvard University Press, 1971), 92. Rawls includes social goods (e.g. rights and liberties), natural goods (e.g. health and vigour), basic liberties, and self-respect. Blustein argues that parents have an obligation to supply their children's needs, which he defines to encompass the Rawlsian primary goods (Blustein, *Parents and Children*, 120–5): 'Caretakers must protect children's health, develop the physical, emotional, and intellectual competences necessary to rational action, nourish their self-esteem and self-confidence, ready them to take advantage of and responsibly exercise their rights and liberties as citizens, and, as far as possible, provide them with conditions favorable to grasping the educational, occupational, and other opportunities available to them in society' (124–5).

For Blustein, the primary goods are only a guide to the wide-ranging goods, liberties, and rights that children need in order that they, as adults, can pursue their own life plans and achieve some minimum level of well-being. He notes that different parents will weigh 'certain primary goods more than others'. He argues that this is compatible with justice, provided that parents 'secure at least some minimum amount of each of these primary goods of their children' (130).

10. I use the phrase 'basic needs' to refer to the minimum threshold of each of the primary goods needed by a child.

11. J. Rawls, *Political Liberalism* (New York: Columbia University Press, 1993), in particular Lecture 6, section 5: 'The Idea of Constitutional Essentials', 231–40.

12. Schoeman develops a similar definition of the family, and also characterizes the relationship as moral. See F. Schoeman, 'Rights of Children, Rights of Parents, and the Moral Basis of the Family', *Ethics*, 91 (1980), 9–10.

13. These options are discussed by a variety of authors. See, for example, J. Blustein, *Parents and Children*, particularly Part II, Chap. 2: 'The Assignment of Childrearing Duties'. See also L. Houlgate, *Family and State: The Philosophy of Family Law* (Totowa, NJ: Roman and Littlefield, 1988), particularly Chap. 8: 'The Struggle for Custody'.

14. The classic example in modern society is on some Israeli kibbutzim.

15. Many theories abound. For example, Hobbes argued that parental authority is justified by an implicit contract between parents and children. T. Hobbes, *De Corpore Politico* (1640), in R. S. Peter (ed.), *Body, Man and Citizen* (New York: Collier Press, 1967). This view is not popular today. Locke, on the other hand, maintained that parental authority is justified because of the caretaker responsibilities that parents have for their children, which requires that they have the power to

fulfil their duties (Locke, *Two Treatises*, particularly Treatise I). Blustein, in *Parents and Children*, offers a contemporary neo-Lockean approach. A third approach is offered by Schoeman, who argues that the authority is derived from family intimacy. See Schoeman, 'Moral Basis'.

16. F. Schoeman, 'Book Review: *Family and State: The Philosophy of Family Law*, by Laurence D. Houlgate', *Ethics*, 99 (1989), 654.

17. The *Gesellschaft/Gemeinschaft* distinction is credited by most writers to Tönnies (F. Tönnies, *Gemeinschaft und Gesellschaft*, trans. C. P. Loomis as *Community and Society* [East Lansing, Mich.: Michigan State University Press, 1957]) although similar theories existed in the works of Confucius and Plato (Sorokin, Foreword, *Gemeinschaft und Gesellschaft*, p. ix). For Tönnies, *Gemeinschaft* and *Gesellschaft* represented ideal types or mental constructs which were not mutually exclusive in actual practice. Houlgate's theory of the family is based on pure *Gemeinschaft* traits which introduces a dichotomy not consistent with Tönnies's writings. Furthermore, I will argue that even if a group could be based solely on one ideal type, some of the pure *Gemeinschaft* traits are not desirable for families.

18. *In re* Carson, 39 Misc.2d 544, 545, 241 N.Y.S.2d 288, 289 (1962).

19. I say 'ideally' because the earliest cases involved economic decisions made on behalf of individuals who had never been competent. This same error has been perpetuated in medical cases. See, for example, Superintendent of Belchertown State School v. Saikewicz, 373 Mass. 728, 370 N.E.2d 417 (1977).

20. I. Kant, *Grounding for the Metaphysics of Morals* (1785), trans. J. W. Ellington (Indianapolis, Ind.: Hackett Publishing, 1981), paragraph 429.

21. Landesman, for example, argues that the Kantian principle of respect for persons can only apply to full rational persons. See C. Landesman, 'Against Respect for Persons', in O. H. Green (ed.), *Respect for Persons: Tulane Studies in Philosophy*, 31 (1982), 31–43. In contrast, Brody argues that the principle can apply to potential persons, although the amount of respect owed can vary according to the individual's capacities. See B. Brody, *Life and Death Decision Making* (New York: Oxford University Press, 1988), 32–5.

   Downie and Telfer argue that the principle of respect encompasses the attitude of *agape*, which allows the principle to refer to children and other individuals who are not strictly Kantian persons. See R. S. Downie and E. Telfer, *Respect for Persons* (New York: Schocken Books, 1970), esp. 34–5.

22. Landesman and Cranor argue that respect for persons applies to respect for the rights of persons. See Landesman, 'Against Respect',

and C. Cranor, 'Limitations on Respect-for-Persons Theories', in O. H. Green (ed.), *Respect for Persons: Tulane Studies in Philosophy*, 31 (1982), 45–60. In contrast, Brody argues that it applies to respect for the potentials of persons. See B. Brody, 'Towards a Theory of Respect for Persons', in O. H. Green (ed.), *Respect for Persons: Tulane Studies in Philosophy*, 31 (1982), 61–76.

23. Telfer and Downie argue that respect for persons is *the* fundamental moral principle. See Telfer and Downie, *Respect for Persons*.

24. Kant defines persons as rational beings to be distinguished from human beings in general (Kant, *Grounding*). In this book, I use the phrase 'Kantian person' in this technical sense. I also use the phrase 'developing person' based on Brody's definition of a 'potential person'. Brody defines 'potential persons' as 'having the potential to perform a wide variety of actions whose performance we value greatly. These include the potential to make rational (and especially principled) choices, the potential to engage in a variety of interpersonal relations, the potential to appreciate beauty, and the potential to desire to know the truth.' (B. Brody, *Life and Death Decision Making*, 33, footnote omitted.) Most children are 'potential persons' as defined by Brody.

25. R. S. Downie and K. C. Calman, *Healthy Respect: Ethics in Health Care*, 2nd ed. (New York: Oxford University Press, 1994), 72–8. Brody also argues that 'potential persons' deserve respect. He argues for a sliding scale of respect depending on the degree to which one has actualized one's potentials for personhood (Brody, *Life and Death Decision Making*, 34–5).

26. This does not mean that the mentally retarded individual who may never become a Kantian person is not deserving of respect. He or she is, but is owed less than that owed to a fully actualized person. Downie and Calman discuss this in *Healthy Respect*, 72–8. For the purpose of this book, I assume that the child is of normal capabilities unless specifically stated otherwise.

27. Although Telfer and Downie, in *Respect for Persons*, and Downie and Calman, in *Healthy Respect*, acknowledge that a theory of respect for persons would have to be modified to apply to children, they do not explore what modifications would be necessary.

28. I use the terms 'assent' and 'consent' to refer to the incompetent and competent child's agreement to participate respectively. Consent implies that the agreement meets legal standards whereas assent does not. Incompetent children are incapable of giving consent. However, by 'consent' I do not mean to imply that the competent child's consent or refusal needs to be legally binding, only that it meets legal standards.

29. '*Virtually* futile' is the phrase used in many U.S. government documents to refer to cases of low-probability, low-efficacy, or poor quality-of-life judgements. 'Inhumane treatment' is treatment in which the risks, harms, and costs are high, and the benefits to the patient are extremely small or improbable.

2

A Limited Theory of the Family

1. Blustein's Priority Thesis

In the first part of *Parents and Children: The Ethics of the Family*, Jeffrey Blustein constructs a history of the philosophy of the family. He notes that it is complicated by the fact that there is no common meaning of what constitutes a family in the philosophical literature, and by the changing emotional and psychological significance of the family to its members.[1] In the second part of his book, Blustein develops his ethical theory of the family. He begins with a neo-Lockean view of parental authority, which he attempts to extricate from its theological grounding.[2] Whereas Locke held that parents are caretakers for their children and that the duty of parents to care for their children is sanctioned by God, Blustein grounds parental authority in the child's need for care. The child's needs create parental duties which require that parents have the authority to fulfil these needs: 'The family exists to serve the child, not vice versa, and parents have authority over their children only because they need it to carry out their duties to their children.'[3]

The crux of Blustein's theory is the *absolute* priority of parental duties over parental rights. Parental duties derive from the parents' status as guardians of their children and include duties of need-fulfilment and duties of respect. Duties of need-fulfilment are duties to protect a child's physical, emotional, and psychological development. In contrast, duties of respect are duties 'to respect a child's own desires and wants in matters not critical to protecting the child's basic interests'.[4] The primary rationale for duties of respect is *not* that they are necessary for healthful development but that it is *always* wrong to deprive an individual of freedom 'unless one has adequate justification for doing so'.[5] Although many children are not fully autonomous, Blustein denies that this adequately justifies constraining their autonomy:

'[C]hildren should have as much freedom as is compatible with their present needs, the long-range objectives of parenting, and the safety of others.'[6] Parental rights, on the other hand, accord parents certain freedoms and powers derived from their status as parents (i.e. the freedom to raise their children according to their own conception of the good life) as well as the rights to fulfil their non-parental interests. But Blustein's thesis is that all parental duties (both duties of need-fulfilment and duties of respect) have *absolute* priority over parental rights. This means that parents must fulfil *all* of these duties before they can pursue their own interests.

While the needs and interests of children ought to be central to the goals of the parents, to hold that the needs and interests of children must be given *absolute* priority *at all times and in all circumstances* is untenable. Consider, for example, the following scenario: Amy Smith is a nine-year-old child who has cerebral palsy. If Amy can get better rehabilitation in a large urban setting, then the Smiths may decide to leave their rural community. Alternatively, the Smiths may decide that Amy will have to settle for less-than-optimal medical care. Blustein's priority thesis demands that the Smiths maximize their daughter's rehabilitation. The only justification for not maximizing Amy's rehabilitation is 'if, on balance and over the long run, the welfare of the child is advanced thereby'.[7] For example, the Smiths can choose to remain on the farm *only if* moving would disrupt the family's financial well-being, which would be more detrimental to Amy in the long term (i.e. if Amy's parents are left destitute by the move, then they will not be able to afford *any* care). But the Smiths cannot decide to stay on the farm because the move will impede other goals that the parents find important: their parental duties trump their parental rights.

Blustein's thesis requires that when Amy's interests conflict with those of her parents, Amy's interests must always prevail. In contrast, I will offer a model in which the Smiths' autonomy is respected as long as they satisfy Amy's basic needs. Parents must have the freedom to consider their own needs and interests provided that they have ensured for the provision of their child's basic needs. Parents have (and should have) the autonomy to pursue other goals as long as they have provided their child with adequate care, even if better care is available.

Another problem with Blustein's thesis is that it cannot accommodate families with more than one child. Imagine, for example, that Amy has two sisters. While a move to the city may advance Amy's needs and interests, her sisters' educational and emotional needs may be better satisfied in their rural community. While the move to the city may be best for Amy, all things considered, the move may be detrimental to both her sisters. Even if the Smiths are willing to ignore their own needs and interests, they are unable to satisfy maximally the needs and interests of all their children simultaneously. Blustein's priority thesis offers no solution when the interests of children conflict.

In the third part of *Parents and Children*, Blustein moves away from questions regarding the responsibilities of parents in individual families to questions regarding the institution of the family itself. Because the family is a basic institution of society, Blustein argues that the principles of social justice ought to apply to it.[8] Like John Rawls, Blustein emphasizes the importance of equality of opportunity in a theory of social justice.[9] To the extent that the family interferes with equality of opportunity, Blustein believes that 'justice and the family are incompatible'.[10] Whereas Rawls leaves open the possibility that alternate child-rearing arrangements might prove preferable,[11] Blustein argues that they would not. Blustein argues that eliminating the traditional link between childbearing and child-rearing (i.e. distributing children not on the basis of biology but by another means) will not reduce the inequalities of opportunity because we lack adequate understanding of the relative importance of genetics versus environmental factors on opportunity and how the two interact.[12]

Blustein's solution to diffuse the tension between the family and equal opportunity is similar to the solution advanced by Rawls in *Political Liberalism*. Rawls sought to diffuse the tension by de-emphasizing 'fair *equality* of opportunity' and focusing instead on securing a minimum set of 'constitutional essentials'.[13] Blustein's specific suggestions include the removal of 'negative legal and quasi-legal constraints on equal opportunity . . . [by] providing formal guarantees of nondiscrimination',[14] as well as taking positive steps such as the transfer of resources and the availability of social and educational support services 'to partially equalize the environments of children'.[15]

Blustein is also concerned with injustices at the other end of the spectrum: injustices created when parents go beyond some standard and give their child advantages which other parents are either unable or unwilling to give. Here, then, the question is not whether the Smiths must offer Amy adequate rehabilitation, but whether they can offer Amy's sisters benefits not available to other members of the community so that Amy's sisters can have a head start. Blustein is unwilling to give parents unchecked discretion in giving their children additional benefits beyond a certain level because it conflicts with his egalitarian notion of social justice. Like Michael Walzer in *Spheres of Justice*, Blustein wants to prevent the influence of the family from influencing other spheres like education and job opportunities.[16] Blustein's solution is to support the transfer of many child-rearing responsibilities to other institutions and to retain the family as a more specialized institution of love and intimacy.[17]

Blustein's desire to transfer many child-rearing responsibilities to the community is based on his belief that children 'with similar abilities and motivations [must] have equal chances for culture and educational and occupational achievement'.[18] To the extent that a parent's vision of the good life interferes with a child's procurement of equal opportunity, Blustein would require parents 'to avail themselves of needed support services so that they can provide their children with an environment that affords them access to a full range of future opportunities'.[19]

Blustein's proposal is problematic for those families whose conception of the good life include fewer life plans than those acceptable to their liberal secular counterparts. For example, an Orthodox Jewish parent may not motivate his child to excel in sports particularly if participation in sports conflicts with the Sabbath. His parents are offering him a life plan which coheres with their understanding of the good. While this may handicap their son from getting an athletic scholarship to college, the child does not have a claim against his family to be exposed to a wide range of possible ways of life. Different parents value different life projects, and these values will shape which opportunities they give their children and the extent to which they will emphasize certain skills and talents.[20] Whether parents prepare a child for many lifestyles or only to participate in their own religious or cultural community is part of the diversity that liberalism must respect.[21]

However, some restrictions on parental autonomy are necessary. Parents have an obligation to provide for their children's basic needs. If they do not or cannot, the state should intervene. In deference to the family's need for privacy in order to flourish,[22] the state should limit its intervention to those cases in which the parents fail to provide for the fulfilment of their child's basic needs, not because the parents could provide more.

In summary, Blustein proposes to restrict the family's influence on a child's opportunities by placing a floor and ceiling on the goods and opportunities which parents can offer, provide, or procure for their children. I agree with Blustein that when parents cannot provide their children with a threshold level of primary goods,[23] then the state, as *parens patriae*, is obligated to do so. But to place a ceiling on how far parents can go beyond the threshold minimum unnecessarily restricts parental autonomy. Parents should have a presumptive right to non-interference, a right that is restricted only if they fail to provide for their child's basic needs (i.e. some threshold level of each primary good). My theory will have greater respect for parental and familial autonomy.

2. *Houlgate's Principle of Optimum Communal Benefit*

In *Family and State*, Houlgate offers a theory of the philosophy of family law which 'applies general normative principles or criteria to ethical questions about laws that affect or concern persons insofar as they are members of families'.[24] Houlgate adopts a pure utilitarian approach to evaluate different family law decisions and policies. This contrasts with a previous model that he used in his earlier book, *The Child and the State*. In that work, Houlgate used 'a "mixed" deontological approach that employed the dual standards of utility and justice'.[25] His conception of justice was egalitarian: a distribution was judged just if 'everyone has an equal chance of achieving the best life he is capable of'.[26] But this mixed approach offered him no way to settle conflicts between these principles except by a weak appeal to intuition. Houlgate concedes to his critics,[27] and in his new work he asserts that utility trumps all other principles.[28] However, Houlgate denies the full ramifications of his new thesis.

Houlgate begins *Family and State* by asking, 'How are we to *justify* the existence of families in human society?'[29] He argues in favour of the family partly because of the uniquely intimate nature of family relationships, which give meaning to our lives.[30] Most importantly, though, the family is the locus of child-rearing most conducive to the general happiness.[31]

Houlgate offers a weak utilitarian argument to show that membership in families should be assigned according to a 'biological preference principle', a middle-range principle which supplements the principle of utility:[32]

The argument is based entirely on the peculiar interests of these parents in rearing their own children. Biological parents would undoubtedly experience far more happiness and far less misery under a system that grants them custody of their own children than (say) under a system that awards custody solely on the basis of what candidate for custodian is most likely to promote the best interests of the child. Although the former system may produce less aggregate happiness in those persons who would have enjoyed rearing a child awarded to its biological parent, the amount would (on balance) be a great deal less than the amount of unhappiness that would be produced under the latter system.[33]

To determine which kind of family is *most* conducive to general happiness, Houlgate examines three possible models. According to the organic model, the family is analogous to a biological organism.[34] Parts of an organism exist for the whole and have no interests apart from those related to serving the entire organism. Analogously, in an organic model of the family, family members exist only to serve the family and they lose their individual identities and interests. Houlgate rejects this model because it denies that individual members can have goals apart from those of the family. Rather, he holds that a theory of the family must respect the individual rights of each member.[35]

In the individualistic model, the family is viewed as a corporate partnership. Individual family members are perceived as separate atoms who are 'basically complete apart from the family'.[36] The family is valued to the extent that it helps promote the individual goals of its members. Although this model respects the individual rights and identity of each member, Houlgate rejects it because the source of all obligations are purely contractual. He argues that this model fails to capture the internal source of meaning and obligations unique to intimate relationships.[37]

Houlgate's third model is the communal model which defines the family as a pure community (*Gemeinschaft*), which contrasts with the conception of the family (group) as an organization (*Gesellschaft*) in three distinct ways:

1. communities are groups 'without goals';

2. communities are groups 'unable to act and make decisions in the way that organizations act and make decisions';

3. communities are groups whose members are related to others in an 'internal' rather than an 'external' way; that is, the members are related by intimate relationships and not by a 'third something' such as a contract or shared end.[38]

The notion of the family as a pure community contradicts John Ladd's theory, on which Houlgate's theory is based. Ladd used the terms *Gemeinschaft* and *Gesellschaft* to represent ideal-types and not to describe any actual group, past or present.[39] In fact, Ladd specifically denied that any actual group does or could embody the pure concept of *Gemeinschaft*.[40] I will return to this issue in section 3 below.

Houlgate's thesis is that public policies that rely on the communal model are most conducive to the general happiness because under the communal model, families can function as child-rearing groups that (1) provide children with a 'psychological parent';[41] (2) provide children and parents with a source of intimacy; (3) locate the significance of the family internally; and simultaneously, (4) do not deny individual family members their basic civil rights.[42] Houlgate incorporates this model of the family into a middle-range principle called the principle of optimum communal benefit. This principle states that 'when two or more laws are proposed as a response to a problem concerning families, then we are to choose or prefer the law that has the most beneficial effect on the ability of families to function as communities'.[43]

Ferdinand Schoeman criticizes the use of a utilitarian calculus to judge the family because it values the family only to the extent that it promotes optimal welfare and ignores the intrinsic value of the family.[44] Houlgate's position would support the dissolution of the family if another family or institution could be formed that would have greater utility: '[W]hen the principle of optimal communal benefit conflicts with utility, we must opt for utility.'[45] Although Houlgate believes 'that cases in which utility dictates this sort of override are extremely rare',[46] Schoeman objects that Houlgate's approach fails to capture the reasons why families matter. It requires Houlgate to justify parental authority solely on the grounds that parents are in the best position to promote their child's welfare.[47] While Schoeman agrees that parental authority generally promotes the child's welfare and that this is a good reason to permit parental authority, he denies that it is the only justification.[48] Rather, parental authority can also be justified because the family is an important social institution which gives meaning to the lives of adults as well as children. Houlgate fails to give any value to the interests that adults may have in child-bearing and child-rearing that do not benefit the child directly.

The remainder of Houlgate's book is a utilitarian critique of current public policies that affect the structure or function of families. By using the principle of utility and several middle-range principles (e.g. the biological preference principle and the principle of optimum communal benefit), Houlgate attempts to show how the communal-model family offers the most appropriate solutions regarding family law. Some of his conclusions would require modest changes, others would require radical reform. They include a two-track system of conjugal partnership depending upon whether the couple plans to have children, the elimination of rules that permit individuals to prevent spouses from testifying against them in criminal trials, and the rejection of the best interest standard as the basis for state intervention in favour of a more limited 'protectable harms' doctrine. Unfortunately, many of his suggestions entail greater state scrutiny and intervention than he imagines.

Consider the following example. Houlgate argues that parental refusals of medical care should be overridden only if the refusal places the child at serious risk. He uses the case of Kevin Sampson as an illustration.[49] Kevin Sampson was a sixteen-year-old with neurofibromatosis, a condition that caused large disfiguring tumors to develop on his face. The tumors were not life-threatening, but were severely disfiguring and school officials prohibited Kevin from attending school because his appearance was disruptive. Kevin's mother agreed to surgery, but refused transfusions on religious grounds. The physicians argued that the surgery could not be done without transfusions, and so they took Mrs Sampson to court claiming that she was medically neglectful of her child. The judge agreed with the physicians, adding that the disfigurement 'must inevitably exert a most negative effect upon his personality development'.[50]

Three facts must be emphasized. First, the tumors were not life-threatening. Second, arguments were presented that the surgery was risky and could be performed with less risk at an older age. Third, the staff psychiatrist who examined Kevin found 'no evidence of any thinking disorder' and that 'in spite of marked facial disfigurement he failed to show any outstanding personality aberration'.[51]

Houlgate agreed with the court that Kevin's mother's refusal was neglectful. Her failure to provide for his basic medical needs resulted in the failure of procuring his basic educational needs. I disagree. Kevin's medical problems were not life-threatening and his doctors testified that the surgery would be less risky in several years. As such, surgery was not immediately necessary to promote Kevin's basic medical needs. Two options existed to procure Kevin's educational needs that would not override Kevin's mother's religious-based refusal of surgery. First, Kevin should have been allowed to attend school. To discriminate on the basis of physical deformities is immoral and illegal. Second, the school could have offered Kevin in-home tutoring. Since the refusal of surgery did not threaten Kevin's basic medical nor his basic educational needs, the state had no right to intervene.

In summary, Houlgate's utilitarian approach to the family ignores the value of the family, which persists even if other institutions can perform parental duties better, more efficiently, or more justly. In addition, the specific policy recommendations that Houlgate derives from his theory, as exemplified by the Kevin Sampson case, permit state intervention not merely to secure a child's *basic* needs, but also to promote his 'best interest', as defined by the state.[52] My own theory will have greater respect for family intimacy and family autonomy.

3. *An Alternate Theory: A Partial Theory of the Intimate Family*

Houlgate's book raises the important question of what the characteristics are of a family *qua* family that distinguish it from other institutions to which we belong. In particular, I want to consider what the characteristics are of an intimate family. Houlgate defined the optimal family model in terms of the three characteristics of *Gemeinschaft*, that is, a group without goals that is unable to act and make decisions like an organization whose members are related internally. I will examine whether these characteristics are necessary for the family to be intimate.

The first characteristic of a *Gemeinschaft* (community) is that it is a group without goals, whereas a *Gesellschaft* (organization) is created for a specific goal (e.g. a shoe company is formed to manufacture shoes). Ladd specifically denies the possibility that a community can have goals of its own. In fact, he specifically rejects Aristotle's claim that 'every community is established with a view to some good'.[53] Rather, he claims, '[Aristotle's] dictum holds of organizations but not of communities'.[54] Ladd does not mean that members of a community do not have goals in common, but that a community is not formed with a specific goal in mind and that it does not have goals distinct from the goals of its individual members.

Although organizations and communities may exist, develop, and evolve for different purposes, this does not prove that communities are not established with some goal in view. A young couple who decide to marry form a new community. Their decision may reflect their goal to share their lives together, to conceive and rear children together, or to express their mutual love publicly. Although the purposes for the establishment of a marriage and family differ from the purposes for which organizations are formed, they are still formed with some goal in view. In this regard, families do not fit the characteristic of *Gemeinschaft*.

Families can have goals, goals that are distinct from the goals of individual members. Consider a couple with infant twins and several older children. One twin suffers from aplastic anaemia, which is fatal without a bone marrow transplant. The risks and harms associated with a bone marrow donation are not minimal, but are within the realm of risks to which parents often subject their children.[55] For the ill twin, the benefits of the procedure outweigh the risks. From the healthy twin's perspective, the risk/benefit calculation is indeterminate at best. If she does not serve as a donor and her twin dies, she would still have several older siblings and parents, and may not suffer from her twin's death, particularly if she is too young to remember. If she does serve as a donor, and her twin does not survive, then her participation may yield minimal benefit. Even if her twin survives, the benefits may be minimal; for example, the twins may become enemies, the transplant may create economic hardship for the family leaving the healthy twin worse off, or the healthy twin may suffer a serious complication during the bone marrow harvest.

Why do we allow parents to authorize a child's participation as a bone marrow donor? Schoeman, in analysing a similar case, explains:

> In looking at decisions within a family that concern a child, I have suggested that factors other than the parents' responsibility for promoting the child's interests may be taken into account legitimately. These other factors can roughly be characterized as concerns emerging from the desire to promote the *family's welfare or character*. Such a perspective does not entitle parents to sacrifice their children's lives or welfare, although it does permit parents to compromise the child's interests for ends related to *family welfare*. Such a perspective recognizes the child as having a status within the family by virtue of which certain liabilities and responsibilities accrue.[56]

That is, we allow parents to authorize the donation by one sibling to another because it serves family goals. This authorization does not depend upon the child's future consent, nor does it require that the child come to view the donation as in her best interest. Schoeman argues that parents can make decisions that go beyond the best interests of individual members, provided that they do not sacrifice the basic needs of any (child) member.[57] The family can pursue goals that do not coincide with the goals of particular family members, provided that these goals do not require the sacrifice of any of the children's basic needs.[58]

This does not mean that all members of intimate families have the same goals. Individual members have their own particular goals, but as members of an intimate family, they share some common goals and accommodate those goals held by others that they do not share. While members do not necessarily strive to maximize the goals of other family members, they do incorporate each other and the others' goals. Hardwig explains, 'This does not, of course, mean that all interests will be shared, but it means I am interested even in those of your interests I do not share':[59]

In a healthy personal relationship, I do not respect you . . . as an independent being with independent ends that have as much right to fulfillment as my ends. Rather I want you and I want your well-being, and your ends are my ends too. To have you as one of my ends is thus to see you and the realization of your goals as part of me and the realization of my goals.[60]

The second distinction between *Gesellschaft* and *Gemeinschaft* is that organizations can act and make decisions, whereas communities cannot. According to Ladd and Houlgate, it makes sense to say that a shoe company can hire and fire or expand and dissolve itself, but it does not make sense to say that a family has decided to go on vacation.[61] Rather, one can infer that 'certain individuals within the Smith family (such as the parents) have reached this decision'.[62]

What Houlgate and Ladd mean is that a family decision is not a decision of the family as a whole, but is a decision by some of its members imposed on the family as a whole. In contrast, they suggest that a decision by a corporation represents the company as a whole. Generally, this is not the case. The hourly wage employer does not decide whether the company will expand or contract; rather, it is the decision of the owner, the board of directors, or the CEO (depending on the size of the company). Even in a more democratic organization such as a five-partner law firm, majority vote and not unanimity is generally all that is required to decide on the firm's course of action.

Ladd and Houlgate are correct to say that parents usually choose the place, the time, and the type of family vacation. Even if parents try to accommodate the interests of their children, they still make the final decision. But such an interpretation ignores the possibility that the parents are acting not only as agents of themselves but also as agents of the family as a group. It ignores the possibility that within intimate families, one member's well-being is an integral part of the other member's well-being. Intimates take on one another's goals, even as they retain their independent goals and identity.[63] To the extent that each family member incorporates the other members and the other members' ends into his own ends, the difference between altruism and egoism collapses.[64] Other-regarding activities become self-regarding activities.

Like Ladd and Houlgate, Allen Buchanan and Dan Brock

specifically deny that family interests are anything more than the interests of each individual member: '[T]o speak of the family as having its own goals and purposes and to speak of the familial perspective and familial objectives is to engage in dangerous reification.'[65] They argue that decisions by the whole family are really decisions imposed on the family by the parents. Family autonomy collapses into parental autonomy and should not be given special status: 'Given the very great inequality of power between parents and children, reference to the family's interest or "familial objectives" is all too likely to serve as a cover for the parents' interests precisely in those cases in which the latter conflict with those of the child.'[66]

Margaret Steinfels rejects the claim that family autonomy is synonymous with parental autonomy. She points to recent research which

confirms the experience of many parents that 'behavior control' is by no means exclusively in the hands of the adults of the family. Infants have compelling powers to control behavior and elicit responses in adults that can as effectively establish the modus vivendi of family life as any parental theory about infant care and child-rearing.[67]

Schoeman also argues that family autonomy is not synonymous with parental autonomy. He argues that parents can and do make decisions which reflect the needs and interests of the family as a unit:

Parents can be seen as representing the interests of the family as an integrated whole in addition to representing their own particular interests. Though entrusting individuals with the responsibility of making judgments for the common good when their own interests are involved does not accord well with modern constitutionalist conceptions, we should not discount on a priori grounds the prospects for such an arrangement's being feasible in certain contexts. The context in which such kinds of representation can work are those in which people in fact conceive their roles and their very identity as requiring such an attitude.[68]

According to Schoeman, parents in intimate families perceive themselves as representatives of the family's interests, and this identity can be separated from their roles as representatives of their own interests. As such, parents can serve as both moderator and disputant in intimate family decisions.

To maintain that family autonomy is synonymous with

parental autonomy also ignores the influence that children, even infants, have in eliciting responses in adults that can profoundly influence relationship and goals. Although parents have ultimate authority, their decisions are influenced by the needs and interests of children. Parental decisions can reflect a family decision. Again, decision making within an intimate family does not fit Ladd's description of decision making within *Gemeinschaft*.

The third characteristic of *Gemeinschaft* construes individuals as related internally whereas members of organizations require a 'third something' to tie them together.[69] This distinction fails to capture how the identities of some employees become enmeshed with the identity of their company, as is particularly true in Japan,[70] and overlooks that some family relationships are formed by a 'third something', for example, a marriage contract (even if the goal of marriage is to transcend the contract and create a new shared personality).[71] While one need not understand marriage as the surrender of one's whole personality such that the couple becomes a single person, marriage does require the couple to forge a new identity that is not reducible to the personalities of the individual members. To the extent that a couple is unable to transcend the contractual nature of marriage and continues to perceive all their interests and identity as distinctly 'mine' or 'yours' and not 'ours', the couple is not an intimate couple. Intimate couples and intimate family relationships are related internally, but not necessarily exclusively so, as Ladd suggests.

A fourth distinction between *Gemeinschaft* and *Gesellschaft* not raised by Ladd and Houlgate is that the former has intrinsic worth to its members, whereas the latter does not. A shoe company is valued only insofar as it creates a valuable product. If it were to stop producing shoes, its value would be lost, and it would dissolve.[72] An intimate group, however, is valued both for what it does (e.g. the family is valued for its child-rearing functions) and for what it is (e.g. we value the family for its intimate nature). The Smith family continues to exist even after the children are grown and move out of the house. The members continue to derive meaning from their membership, and they continue to be intimately related. However, the Smiths can divorce or they can physically abuse their children. In these cases, intimacy has not lost its value, but the group is no longer intimate.

My analysis of *Gemeinschaft* and *Gesellschaft* illustrates the difficulty in trying to describe the criteria that differentiate an intimate from a non-intimate group.[73] Understood as ideal-types, these concepts can help to provide a preliminary description of an intimate group. An intimate group is a group in which members derive benefit if not identity from membership even after the group's goals are achieved or are no longer important. Members make compromises for each other in order to promote the goals of the group in addition to their individual goals. It is a group in which members try to accommodate one another's needs rather than disengage. This does not mean that intimate groups cannot dissociate, but it calls attention to the significant costs that disengagement entails. In the language of Albert Hirschman, intimate groups such as families are characterized by voice (dialogue and compromise) rather than by exit (separation and divorce). Bonds of loyalty (care and commitment) minimize the risk of defection by individual members, even after the common goals are achieved or no longer desired.[74]

The intimate family is one example of an intimate group. What distinguishes an intimate family with non-emancipated child(ren) from other intimate groups is the parents' obligation to procure (or make provisions for the procurement of) a threshold amount of each primary good for each child member. This model of the intimate family is integral to my decision-making model for children, which I present in the next chapter.

Notes

1. J. Blustein, *Parents and Children: The Ethics of the Family* (New York: Oxford University Press, 1982), 20.
2. Blustein, *Parents and Children*, 112.
3. Blustein, *Parents and Children*, 111.
4. Blustein, *Parents and Children*, 117.
5. Blustein, *Parents and Children*, 117.
6. Blustein, *Parents and Children*, 117.
7. Blustein, *Parents and Children*, 114.
8. Blustein, *Parents and Children*, 200.
9. Blustein, *Parents and Children*, 200–5. See also J. Rawls, *A Theory of Justice* (Cambridge, Mass.: Belknap Press of Harvard University Press, 1971), 74 and 301.

10. Blustein, *Parents and Children*, 200. This conclusion is similar to Rawls's position in *A Theory of Justice*, 511–12.

11. Rawls, *A Theory of Justice*, 463.

12. Blustein, *Parents and Children*, 210–11.

13. J. Rawls, *Political Liberalism* (New York: Columbia University Press, 1993), 228–30.

14. Blustein, *Parents and Children*, 206.

15. Blustein, *Parents and Children*, 128.

16. M. Walzer, *Spheres of Justice: A Defense of Pluralism and Equality* (New York: Basic Books, 1983), 20.

17. Blustein, *Parents and Children*, 217–23. Walzer's solution, in contrast, is to *increase* the role of the family in child-rearing. See Walzer, *Spheres of Justice*, 233, note.

18. Blustein, *Parents and Children*, 127.

19. Blustein, *Parents and Children*, 128.

20. Blustein does not deny this. He realizes that 'equal opportunity must be balanced against the values of intimacy and diversity' (Blustein, *Parents and Children*, 223). But Blustein argues that the present inequalities are too great and should be reduced (Blustein, *Parents and Children*, 128).

21. W. A. Galston, *Liberal Purposes: Goods, Virtues, and Diversity in the Liberal State* (New York: Cambridge University Press, 1991), 251–5.

22. See, for example, F. Schoeman, 'Rights of Children, Rights of Parents, and the Moral Basis of the Family', *Ethics*, 91 (1980), 6–19; and J. Goldstein, A. Freud, and A. Solnit, *Before the Best Interests of the Child*, ii (New York: Free Press, 1979).

23. What this threshold is depends upon the good in question, the overall material and technological status of the community, and the community's 'shared understanding' of the appropriate level of redistribution. I will not argue for any specifics.

24. L. Houlgate, *Family and State: The Philosophy of Family Law* (Totowa, NJ: Rowman and Littlefield, 1988), p. xii.

25. Houlgate, *Family and State*, 185.

26. Houlgate, *Family and State*, 99–100.

27. Houlgate, *Family and State*, 186, note 2.

28. Elsewhere, Houlgate has offered some arguments about why he chose utilitarianism over a deontological, justice-based approach. See L. Houlgate, 'Ethical Theory and the Family', in D. T. Meyers, K. Kipnis, and C. F. Murphy, Jr. (eds.), *Kindred Matters: Rethinking the Philosophy of the Family* (Ithaca, NY: Cornell University Press, 1993), 59–73.

29. Houlgate, *Family and State*, 27.

30. Houlgate, *Family and State*, 35.

31. Houlgate, *Family and State*, 39.

32. Houlgate, *Family and State*, 108. Middle-range principles are neither absolute nor inviolable. If the principle of utility conflicts with a middle-range principle, the principle of utility must prevail (Houlgate, *Family and State*, 16).

33. Houlgate, *Family and State*, 113.

34. Houlgate, *Family and State*, 51.

35. Houlgate, *Family and State*, 51. These rights are not absolute and can be overridden. For Houlgate, rights are middle-range principles which are justified solely on the basis of their utility.

36. Houlgate, *Family and State*, 52.

37. Houlgate, *Family and State*, 51–3.

38. Houlgate, *Family and State*, 37.

39. J. Ladd, 'The Idea of Community', *New England Journal* (an occasional publication of the New England Chapter of the American Institute of Planners), 1 (1972), 8.

40. Ladd, 'The Idea', 8.

41. Houlgate adopts the phrase 'psychological parent' from J. Goldstein, A. Freud, and A. J. Solnit, *Beyond The Best Interests of the Child*, new ed. with epilogue (New York: Free Press, 1979). They define a 'psychological parent' as 'one who, on a continuing, day-to-day basis, through interaction, companionship, interplay and mutuality, fulfills the child's psychological needs for a parent, as well as the child's physical needs' (98).

42. Houlgate, *Family and State*, 33–9.

43. Houlgate, *Family and State*, 49.

44. F. Schoeman, 'Book Review: *Family and State: The Philosophy of Family Law* by Laurence D. Houlgate', *Ethics*, 99 (1989), 651.

45. Schoeman, 'Book Review', 653, paraphrasing Houlgate, *Family and State*, 50.

46. Houlgate, *Family and State*, 50.

47. Houlgate, *Family and State*, 176.

48. Schoeman, 'Book Review', 654.

49. *In re* Sampson, 65 Misc.2d 658, 317 N.Y.S.2d 641 (Fam. Ct. 1970) *aff'd*, 37 App. Div.2d 668, 323 N.Y.S.2d 253 (1971), *aff'd*, 29 N.Y.2d 900, 278, N.E.2d 918, 328 N.Y.S.2d 686 (1972).

50. *In re* Sampson, 65 Misc.2d at 660, 317 N.Y.S.2d at 641.

51. See the discussion of *In re Sampson* by Goldstein, Freud, and Solnit, *Before the Best Interests of the Child*, 101–5.

52. Although I reject the idea that parents must promote their child's best interest, this case brings up a different issue: Who defines what is in a child's best interest? I believe that parents have the right and responsibility to define their child's best interest because they decide which primary goods they will emphasize and to what degree. Of

course, their autonomy is not unchecked. However, in this case, the state decided that it was in Kevin's best interest to have the surgery, although there are strong arguments to support the position that it was in his best interest to defer the surgery.

53. See Ladd, 'The Idea', 29, criticizing Aristotle's position in the *Politics* (Book 1, Chap. 1), 1252a1.

54. Ladd, 'The Idea', 29.

55. I address the issue of risk and the degree of risk to which parents can subject their children in Chapter 6.2.

56. F. Schoeman, 'Parental Discretion and Children's Rights: Background and Implications for Medical Decision-Making', *Journal of Medicine and Philosophy*, 10 (1985), 57 (emphasis added).

57. Whether a decision *compromises* or *sacrifices* a child's basic needs depends upon whether the risks and harms of the decision are expected to leave the child's basic needs filled or unfilled (that is, above or below the threshold that every child is entitled to). The distinction depends upon expected risks and benefits and entails line-drawing. In the second half of this book, I offer proposals as to where these lines should be drawn in various health care settings.

58. Although I believe that a parent should be able to make a decision to voluntarily sacrifice her own basic needs, such a discussion goes beyond the scope of this book.

59. J. Hardwig, 'In Search of an Ethics of Personal Relationships', in G. Graham and H. LaFollette (eds.), *Person to Person* (Philadelphia, Pa.: Temple University Press, 1989), 63–81, esp. 65.

60. J. Hardwig, 'Should Women Think in Terms of Rights?', *Ethics*, 94 (1984), 445.

61. See Houlgate, *Family and State*, 36, and Ladd, 'The Idea', 29.

62. Houlgate, *Family and State*, 36.

63. Hardwig, 'In Terms of Rights?', 445.

64. Hardwig, 'In Terms of Rights?', 445–6.

65. A. E. Buchanan and D. W. Brock, *Deciding for Others: The Ethics of Surrogate Decision Making* (New York: Cambridge University Press, 1989), 236.

66. Buchanan and Brock, *Deciding for Others*, 237.

67. M. O. Steinfels, 'Children's Rights, Parental Rights, Family Privacy and Family Autonomy', in W. Gaylin and R. Macklin (eds.), *Who Speaks for the Child: The Problems of Proxy Consent* (New York: Plenum Press, 1982), 253.

68. Schoeman, 'Rights of Children, Rights of Parents', 19.

69. Ladd, 'The Idea', 30.

70. To the extent that one's identity becomes enmeshed with one's company is the extent to which the workplace plays a role greater than

that of a source of employment. The workplace begins to take on some of the characteristics more common of *Gemeinschaft*. This is further support that *Gesellschaft* and *Gemeinschaft* are ideal-types and not actual descriptions of actual organizations or communities respectively.

71. G. W. F. Hegel, *Philosophy of Right* (1821), trans. with notes by T. M. Knox (New York: Oxford University Press, 1967), paragraph 163.

72. Again, to the extent that one's identity becomes enmeshed with one's company is the extent to which the workplace takes on some of the characteristics more common of *Gemeinschaft*. It is also possible that subgroups develop within an organization from which its members derive value long after the organization dissolves. Members of several World War II units continue to derive value from their membership more than fifty years after the end of the war.

73. The problem with attempting to define a concept such as intimacy is comparable to the problem faced by the Supreme Court in *Jacobellis v. Ohio*. There, in reference to defining 'hard-core pornography', Justice Potter Stewart wrote: 'I shall not today attempt to define [that category] and perhaps I could never succeed in intelligibly doing so. But I know it when I see it.' Jacobellis v. Ohio 378 U.S. 184 (1964), cited in J. Feinberg, *The Moral Limits of the Criminal Law*, ii: *Offense to Others* (New York: Oxford University Press, 1985), 297. The characteristics that define an intimate family merits its own book-length analysis. But the family should be assumed intimate, which makes specific and exclusive criteria less important. A family should be classified as non-intimate only as a last resort.

74. See A. O. Hirschman, *Exit, Voice and Loyalty: Responses to Decline in Firms, Organizations and States* (Cambridge, Mass.: Harvard University Press, 1970).

3

Constrained Parental Autonomy

1. Surrogate Decision Making

In *Deciding for Others: The Ethics of Surrogate Decision Making*, Allen Buchanan and Dan Brock seek to determine how decisions ought 'to be made for those who are not competent to decide for themselves'.[1] They break down the question into four subquestions: (1) What values should be promoted by surrogate decision makers? (2) Who should the surrogate decision maker be? (3) What guiding principles should the surrogates adhere to? and (4) When and by whom should the surrogate's decision be overridden?

Buchanan and Brock argue that surrogates should be guided in their decision making by a 'patient-centered' focus by which they mean 'that considerations of the incompetent's own well-being and (where possible) self-determination, as opposed to the interests of others should be the primary focus'.[2] When the incompetent is a child, they add a *'third substantial value . . .* the interest of the *parents* in making important decisions about the welfare of their minor children', which they note is an important factor 'that has not been sufficiently appreciated in the literature . . . or in health care practice'. [3]

Buchanan and Brock state that parents should be their child's surrogate decision maker both because children need a surrogate and because parents have a legitimate interest in making decisions for their children. They give four reasons to support their position:

1. 'Because in most cases parents both care deeply about the welfare of their children and know them and their needs better than others do, they will be more concerned as well as better able than anyone else to ensure that the decisions made will serve their children's welfare.'

2. 'Parents bear the consequences of treatment choices for their dependent children and so should have at least some control of those choices.'

3. 'A right of parents, at least, within limits, to raise their children according to the parents' own standards and values and to seek to transmit those standards and values to their children.'

4. 'Family is a valuable social institution, in particular [in] its role in fostering intimacy. . . . [This requires freedom,] and one aspect of this freedom or privacy is the right, at least within limits to make important decisions about the welfare of its incompetent members.'[4]

Buchanan and Brock next consider the three most popular guiding principles for surrogate decision making: advance directives, substituted judgement, and the best interest standard.[5] Advance directives, such as living wills, are executed by competent patients to determine what actions should be taken on their behalf if they should become incompetent. Advance directives emphasize respect for the patient's autonomy. Substituted judgement is a principle by which a surrogate is supposed to act according to how the incompetent individual would act if he were competent. Here also there is an emphasis on the competent patient's autonomy. The best interest standard, on the other hand, requires the surrogate to act so as to maximally promote the patient's good. This principle is valid even if the patient has never been competent or if his personal wishes are unknown. Buchanan and Brock argue that because children have never been competent, the best interest standard is the most appropriate guidance principle.[6]

Lastly, Buchanan and Brock ask which authorities should intervene and on what grounds they should do so. They argue that who should intervene depends upon the setting in which the decision occurs. Health care decisions, for example, can be challenged by any member of the health care team, but they should not be challenged by an uninvolved third party.[7] Suspicions of child abuse and neglect, on the other hand, can be raised by anyone in direct contact with the child (e.g. teacher, clergyman, family physician, or neighbour) who has specific reason to believe that the child's well-being is endangered.

The grounds for intervention, according to Buchanan and Brock, include three types of cases. The first includes those that disqualify the parents as surrogates. For example, parents who abuse or neglect their child, parents who are themselves incompetent, or parents who have 'a serious conflict of interest which is likely to bias their decision against the patient's rights and interests'.[8] The second includes cases deserving *special scrutiny* 'by virtue of the especially vulnerable position of the incompetent patient, the momentousness of the consequences of the decision, and/or the especially high likelihood of conflicts of interest between patients and surrogates'.[9] The example offered by Buchanan and Brock is organ donations by incompetents. The third type of case focuses on the substance of the decisions. For example, the treatment 'must be within the range of medically sound alternatives as determined by appropriate medical community standards'.[10]

Just as important as the question of what constitutes compelling reasons to intervene is the question of when the reasons to intervene are inadequate. Buchanan and Brock make it clear that failure on the part of parents to maximize their child's best interest is not an adequate reason to intervene: '[T]he best interest principle is to serve only as a regulative ideal, not as a strict and literal requirement, because parents' obligations toward their other children as well as their own legitimate self-interests can conflict with doing what *maximizes* the child's well-being, and sometimes may take precedence over it.'[11] They assert the importance of respect for parental autonomy, even if the parents' decision is not the best decision possible. Although they encourage parents to promote their child's best interest, they argue that it is against the child's interests for the state to compel parents to do so. Instead, they limit state intervention to cases in which the parents are failing (or suspected of failing) to promote the child's basic needs.[12]

Buchanan and Brock define the child's best interest quite narrowly. They assert that the only interests the surrogate should consider are the self-regarding interests of the child.[13] They do not deny that the child may have other-regarding interests, but, they argue:

[i]f there were sufficiently weighty evidence that the individual did take a strong enough interest in the good of others to justify a decision that runs contrary to the patient's self-regarding interests, then this evidence would presumably be strong enough to justify the use of substituted judgment instead of the best interest principle. It appears, then, that when decision-makers must rely on the best interest principle (rather than an advance directive or substituted judgment), the determination should focus on the individual's self-regarding interests, not upon his or her alleged interests in the good of others.[14]

To assume that an individual's interests are purely self-regarding denies the intimate web in which an individual leads her life, and in which the interests of other family members become part of her own interests (as well as the fact that she shares with these other family members some family goals which are not reducible to their individual goals). In this passage, Buchanan and Brock overlook what is integral to intimate familial relationships; although individual family members have their own particular interests and ends, there may exist family goals which can conflict with the self-regarding interests of individual members (provided that they do not override their basic needs). If parents were permitted to consider only their child's self-regarding interests, they would be forced to ignore some of the most important interests and goals that they and their child share as an intimate family. Buchanan and Brock concede this point. Later in their book they qualify their commitment to the best interest standard as a guidance principle by stating that it 'is to serve only as a regulative ideal, not as a strict and literal requirement'.[15]

Yet Buchanan and Brock fail to address the intimate family as a group. Rather, they maintain that 'to speak of the family as having its own goals and purposes and to speak of the familial perspective and familial objectives is to engage in dangerous reification'.[16] In the next section, I show that their failure to accommodate the family as an intimate group undermines their approach to decision making for children.

2. *Parental Decision Making Reconsidered*

Buchanan and Brock argue that the appropriate guidance principle for parents with respect to their children is the best interest standard. According to this standard, parents should not be guided by the child's wishes but are supposed to weigh all relevant factors and decide what is in the child's best interest, all things considered. They maintain that the surrogate should focus solely on 'the current and future interests of the incompetent individual'.[17]

This focus is too narrow. Exclusive focus on the child does not give enough weight to the child's family with whom his interests are inextricably bound. It ignores the intimate family as a community with its own goals. Decision making must focus on individuals *qua* individuals and *qua* members of communities. Any standard which requires exclusive focus on an individual separate from his community memberships cannot adequately accommodate individuals who are members of intimate families.

Because families can have interests that are not reducible to the interests and needs of particular members, parents must be allowed to make intrafamilial trade-offs.[18] This does not mean that parents can sacrifice the basic needs of any child member, but it does mean that parents need not maximize the procurement of primary goods for their children. Parents must fulfil the basic needs of *each* child member; beyond that, parental autonomy ought to be respected.

Consider, for example, when parents seek to authorize their child's participation as a bone marrow donor for a sibling. The main risks to the donor are anaesthesia (rare but potentially life-threatening) and pain (which is temporary). The main benefits to the donor are the benefit he gets from his sibling's survival and any benefit he gets from his altruistic behaviour and its related praise. However, the potential donor may dislike his sibling and deny that he will derive any psychological benefit. His parents may argue that he will benefit in the long term. They may be right; but it is also possible that the donor never benefits. If parents are only allowed to make decisions that advance each child's welfare independently, then the decision to authorize a healthy sibling to serve as a bone marrow donor for his sibling is not necessarily permissible.

This risk/benefit calculation ignores the benefits to the family as a group. From the family's perspective, it is best, all things considered, for the bone marrow transplant to occur. Even if the donor does not procure any direct personal benefit, it is in the interest of the family as a whole (of which the donor is a member) to prevent the sick child's death when help is available at a minor increase over minimal risk. To hold parents to a best interest standard which cannot accommodate intrafamilial trade-offs is to misunderstand the role of parents and the value of the intimate family. Although parents are their children's primary caretakers, '[t]he point of an intimate relationship is not just to supply some necessary ingredient in a needy child's life. The relationship within a family typically has an inner focus and an independent meaning which results from sharing of life and its intimacies.'[19] Parents not only serve to promote the material needs of the child, but they also relate to the child in an intimate interdependence which allows them to act for the well-being of the family as well as the well-being of each child. When the self-regarding interests and goals of a child conflict with the group goals of the family, the parents may compromise the interests of the child, provided that they do not sacrifice the child's basic needs. To deny that parents can consider the common goals of the intimate family is to deny much of what gives our lives meaning.

3. *An Alternate Guidance Principle*

I propose an alternate guidance principle for parents based on a principle of respect for persons rather than the best interest standard. I begin with Baruch Brody's interpretation of Kant's principle of respect for persons. Kant's second version of the categorical imperative states: 'Act in such a way that you treat humanity, whether in your own person or in the person of another, always at the same time as an end and never simply as a means.'[20] According to Brody, respect for persons refers to respect for certain characteristics or potential characteristics of persons. Respect is shown by not interfering in the development and expression of these characteristics:

We think of persons as having the potential to perform a wide variety of actions whose performance we value greatly. These include the potential to make rational (and especially principled) choices, the potential to engage in a variety of interpersonal relations, the potential to appreciate beauty, and the potential to desire to know the truth. We therefore value the person who has those potentials. However there are conditions that are necessary for (or at least facilitate) a person's ability to fulfill these potentials: the person must be alive, must maintain his or her bodily integrity, must be free to make choices and act upon them, and so on. To show respect for persons is to value them by refraining from eliminating those conditions and by acting to promote their presence.[21]

To the extent that children have these potentials, they deserve respect.

An important contribution made by Brody's analysis is the distinction between respect for persons and respect for the rights of persons. Brody explains that if it is morally wrong to maim someone who offers you a large payment in return, it cannot be wrong on a rights-based account when the individual has waived her rights. Nor can it be wrong on the grounds that the right not to be maimed is inalienable because a doctor does not violate a person's rights if he surgically amputates a diseased leg with the patient's consent. Rather, Brody argues:

> The alternative account which I would like to suggest is that the acceptance of these offers is wrong just because that acceptance shows a lack of respect for persons which they deserve just because they are persons. Even if the rights of the person in question are not infringed upon because he has waived these rights, we would still be acting wrongly if we accepted these offers because the acceptance is disrespectful of persons.[22]

Three important conclusions can be derived from Brody's explanations. First, 'respect for persons', unlike 'respect for the rights of persons', is inalienable. Second, respect is independent of consent. Persons cannot waive their respect because it is owed to them on the basis of their humanity, which is inalienable. Third, children, at least potentially, have the characteristics of persons. As such, they are owed respect, even if they are unable to demand it.

Brody's theory of respect goes further in ways that may not be consistent with Kant. Brody argues that there are gradations in the amount of respect due to an individual. Respect is not an all-or-nothing phenomenon, but is owed to individuals proportionate to their potential to perform those actions that we value: '[T]he respect which is owed . . . may vary according to the capacities of the individual in question.'[23] I call this feature the criterion of proportionate respect.[24]

The criterion of proportionate respect does not imply that one should vary the respect shown to competent adults on the basis of their intelligence or accomplishments, but that we should show greater respect to a competent adult (whose potentials are actualized) than to an adult who is no longer competent. With regard to children, we should show greater respect for the goals and values of a mature sixteen-year-old than for the goals and values of an immature six-year-old. In part, it is because the sixteen-year-old has actualized more of the capacities that we value in persons. This does not mean that it is always wrong to override the adolescent's plans or that it is always acceptable to override the young child's, only that greater deference should be given when one considers overriding the adolescent's goals.

Another feature of respect that is necessary if respect is to be useful in personal relationships is a criterion of relational respect which states that what respect allows *and* requires depends upon the agents' relationship.[25] The content of respect owed to individuals varies depending upon the relationship between the individual showing respect and the individual to whom respect is due. For example, whereas it may be sufficient if a stranger does not harm a child, a parent has the positive obligation to help the child become an autonomous adult. This requires that parents fulfil their child's basic needs to the best of their abilities, or arrange for other institutions to do so.

Relational respect also implies that what is permitted and required by various individuals towards each other will vary during an individual's life span and will vary depending upon the circumstances. What it means to respect a professor active in his career is different from that due to a retired professor who suffers from Alzheimer's disease. And what respect requires from his former colleagues is different from what respect requires from his family. The contrasts are even greater with respect to children, whose memberships are less voluntary, whose capacities are less well defined, and whose goals are still evolving. Respect for children requires respect for their present projects, but not to the extent that we would respect these projects if they were the goals of a competent adult. Rather, respect for children requires that parents and other appropriate surrogates not only promote their children's present interests and goals but also guide their children's future interests, projects, and goals.

Sometimes the child's present identity and goals may conflict with those that the parents would like the child to develop. Parents may choose to not respect their child's present goals to promote alternate values and goals because it is their responsibility and privilege to do so. For example, parents may require their child to attend religious school and church services over the child's objection. Even if the child never adopts his parents' religious values, his parents had a right and a responsibility to try to imbue him with their conception of the good. However, one cannot always justify overriding a child's present goals to promote a particular vision of who and what the child should become. I will explore this further in Chapter 4.

A modified principle of respect must incorporate these three criteria: (1) respect is owed to all individuals on the basis of the individual's personhood (and developing personhood); (2) respect is owed proportionate to the actualized capacities of the individual and his or her potential to attain full personhood; and (3) respect varies depending upon the relationship between the subject and the recipient to whom respect is owed. One can begin to understand what it means to treat children with respect by modifying Kant's second formulation of the categorical imperative so as to apply to children: 'Children should never be treated *solely* as a means, but always at the same time, as developing persons and as individuals who have actualized some of the characteristics associated with personhood.' This modified principle includes two overlapping components:

1. a negative component which holds universally and prohibits the abuse, neglect, and exploitation of *all* children;

2. a positive component which only holds in particular relationships and compels particular individuals to provide particular children with the goods, skills, liberties, and opportunities necessary to become autonomous adults capable of devising and implementing their own life plans.

Consider, first, the negative component. On one level, the requirements seem obvious: no one can abuse or neglect children. But when we ask what it means to abuse or neglect a child, we realize that this depends upon the relationship of the child and the adult. For example, in our society, it is abusive for a teacher to take a nap with her student; but it is not abusive if the student is her daughter. In part, the difference is based on cultural norms; in part, the difference is based on what we understand to be the motive. Likewise, it is neglectful for a parent not to provide her child with lunch or lunch money, but no one expects this of her teacher.

The positive component, on the other hand, applies only to particular individuals in relationship to the child. For example, the child's parents are obligated to help the child become an autonomous agent who can implement and devise his own life plans. They are obligated to procure (or provide for the procurement of) their child's basic needs. But this does not imply that children have a claim against their parents (or against those individuals whom their parents choose to help them provide for their child's primary goods) to be exposed to a wide array of lifestyles. Rather, the positive component permits wide parental autonomy in directing their child's future according to their own perception of the good. The claim that a child has 'a right to an open future'[26] is self-contradictory; such a right necessarily precludes certain lifestyles which can be achieved only by restricting the child's exposure.

For example, Amish parents restrict their child's formal education in order to limit their child's exposure to modern technology, foreign cultures, and alternate lifestyles in order that the child will choose to live the life as a farmer in a traditional society. This does not mean that Amish parents can brainwash their child to accept their conception of the good as his own, nor can they deny their child a certain threshold level of any primary good. As Justice White explained in *Wisconsin v. Yoder*, it was one thing that the Amish sought to remove their children from high school. Had they sought an exemption from all schooling, Justice White suggested that the Supreme Court might have found differently because a blanket exemption from all formal education would have threatened the children's development of basic educational skills necessary to implement many different life plans:

This would be a very different case for me if respondents' claim were that their religion forbade their children from attending any school at any time and from complying in any way with the educational standards set by the State. Since the Amish children are permitted to acquire the *basic* tools of literacy . . . I conclude that respondents claim must prevail. . . . Parents cannot impede the normal physical, intellectual and emotional development of their children. If parents do not fulfill their child's *basic* interests, they waive their right to be their child's surrogate voice.[27]

Using the terminology of respect, Justice White's concern is that a blanket exemption from all schooling would be inconsistent with the positive component of the principle of respect that parents owe to children.

That some parents provide their children with a highly competitive private education and that other parents only seek to provide their children with an adequate education is not inherently unjust. Parents will place different emphases on different primary goods. Walzer examines distributional inequalities of particular primary goods and argues that distributional inequalities in different spheres can be just in a liberal pluralistic society in which there is no agreed upon conception of the good.[28] What is essential for justice is that discrepancies in particular spheres (e.g. education, job opportunities, familial love) are relatively independent and that power in one sphere cannot be converted into another.[29]

As long as there is no agreed-upon definition of the good, the decision by some parents to send their child to Exeter (an exclusive boarding school in New England) and the decision of an Amish family to remove their child from formal education at age fourteen are both consistent with the positive component of respect because both parental decisions provide for a threshold level of education. This does not mean that the Exeter graduate and the Amish child will have similar opportunities; only that both sets of parents are providing their children with the goods, skills, liberties, and opportunities necessary to devise and implement particular life plans. Neither offers the child 'an open future': while the Amish child is only prepared for a simple agricultural lifestyle and would flounder in contemporary metropolitan society, the Exeter graduate is able to pursue higher education and technologically related opportunities but would flounder in an Amish community. Although the Exeter graduate has more options, more is not necessarily better. Given that there is no consensus on what the good life entails, parents in a liberal society must be free to choose whether to expose their child to a wide or narrow array of coherent life plans.

This example illustrates the flexibility that parents should have in procuring primary goods for their children. The positive component of the modified principle of respect requires that parents procure a threshold level of each primary good for their child, but beyond that, parents can consider not only the child's self-interests but also the interests of the child as a member of a particular family and community.

Consider, again, the earlier example in which Amy Smith needs physical rehabilitation. The Smiths may decide not to optimize Amy's rehabilitation because of the high cost that moving to the city would have on other interests of other family members. If family goals are integral to Amy's well-being, then the failure to maximize her rehabilitation is offset by the promotion of other aims and ends important to her. Even if Amy presently denies sharing her family's goals, her parents may choose to remain on the farm and their decision is consistent with both components of the modified principle of respect. Amy is not being medically neglected; she is getting good rehabilitation, although better rehabilitation is available.[30] The Smiths do not need to optimize Amy's medical well-being; rather, they can balance her medical needs with her need for other primary goods and with the needs and interests of other family members. The modified principle of respect is a guidance principle which respects the freedom of parents to balance the competing claims of family members, provided that each child-member's basic needs are satisfied.[31] As such, it allows the Smiths to pursue family goals, and to make trade-offs among the needs and interests of Amy and other family members.

4. *Constrained Parental Autonomy*

I propose a model of surrogate decision making for children which is based on parental autonomy constrained by the principle of respect for persons modified to apply to children which I call 'constrained parental autonomy'. A major difference between this model and one based upon the best interest standard is that this model can accommodate intrafamilial trade-off provided that the basic needs of each child member is secured. This difference significantly alters the answers that Buchanan and Brock provide for the four questions which make up their framework for surrogate decision making.

Buchanan and Brock argue that parents are the appropriate surrogate decision makers for their children and that parents should be guided by the child's well-being, the child's self-determination, and the interests of the parents. I agree that parents are the appropriate surrogate decision makers and should be guided by the values enumerated. But I believe that parents are also appropriately guided by family interests, even those interests which are not necessarily reducible to the interests of the individual family members, as long as these interests do not prevent the parents from fulfilling each child's basic needs.

The guidance principle proposed by Buchanan and Brock is the best interest standard. I argued that this standard is too restrictive for intimate families as it does not allow parents to make intrafamilial trade-offs or to consider the interests of the family as an entity. In contrast, a modified principle of respect allows parents to make intrafamilial trade-offs according to their own conception of the good provided that each child's basic needs are procured. Although the different guidance principles will often produce similar results, the modified principle of respect better reflects the central role that families play in our lives.[32]

The last question that Buchanan and Brock considered is when to intervene. They propose that different authorities should be empowered to intervene in different circumstances, depending upon the parents' decision, and they enumerate three sets of cases in which intervention is appropriate. I contend that although families should be accountable to other institutions, there should be great reservation about scrutinizing the intimate family, and that Buchanan and Brock permit too much scrutiny and intervention. For example, they recommend that all decisions by parents to authorize a child to serve as an organ donor for a sibling should be subject to judicial review.[33] This is consistent with their position that parents should make decisions which solely reflect their child's self-regarding interests, and that they should not balance their child's interests with the well-being of other family members or with the well-being of the family as a whole. In contrast, I argue in Chapter 6 that parents in intimate families should be the presumptive decision makers for intrafamilial donations that entail no more than a minor increase over minimal risk, and that judicial scrutiny should be reserved for those donations in which children are to serve as donors to intimate non-familial recipients.

To find exceptions to Buchanan and Brock's intervention guidelines does not negate their value, even if they are prone to counter-examples. Although I will not attempt to prove it, the cases in the second half of the book illustrate that when parents are guided by the modified principle of respect for persons, the need for such a broad set of intervention guidelines is decreased.

Notes

1. A. E. Buchanan and D. W. Brock, *Deciding for Others: The Ethics of Surrogate Decision Making* (Cambridge: Cambridge University Press, 1989), 1. For present purposes, I assume that children are incompetent and do not (and should not) have autonomy in the health care arena. In the next chapter I will consider what modifications, if any, are necessary if children are competent. Competency and autonomy are related but they are not co-extensive. Competency refers to the capacity to understand and voluntarily perform a specific function. Autonomy refers to the freedom or right to act voluntarily. In Chapter 4, I argue that competency is necessary but not sufficient to require respect for a child's autonomy.
2. Buchanan and Brock, *Deciding for Others*, 10.
3. Buchanan and Brock, *Deciding for Others*, 226.
4. Buchanan and Brock, *Deciding for Others*, 233–4. The reasons offered for giving parents presumptive decision-making authority can be grouped as child-centred (1), parent-centred (2 and 3), and family-centred (2, 3, and 4). That is, selecting parents to serve as their child's decision makers serves to promote the interests of the child, the parents, and the family as a whole. This is noteworthy because Buchanan and Brock reject the reification of the family as an entity of its own, which I discuss in the text accompanying note 16 below. I discuss the significance of the family as an entity, an intimate group, in section 2 below.
5. Buchanan and Brock, *Deciding for Others*, 93–6.
6. Although this decision may seem intuitively obvious, the fact is that courts have applied the principle of substituted judgement in cases involving never-competent adults and young children. See, for example, Superintendent of Belchertown State School v. Saikewicz, 373 Mass. 728, 370 N.E.2d 417 (1977) (a case of whether to refuse life-preserving treatment for a never-competent adult), and Hart v. Brown, 29 Conn. Supp. 368, 289 A.2d 386 (Super. Ct. 1972) (a case of whether to allow a seven-year-old child to serve as a kidney donor).

7. This policy has been validated by the New York State Court of Appeals in the case of Baby Jane Doe, a newborn with spina bifida and related complications whose parents refused to authorize surgery on her behalf. An out-of-state lawyer with no relationship to the child, family, medical staff, or hospital filed suit to force surgery on the child. Although the state trial court authorized the surgery, the New York Court of Appeals overturned the decision because it found that the lawyer's action did not comply with state law which required that child neglect proceedings originate with local child protective agencies or by a person on the court's direction. See Weber v. Stony Brook Hospital, 467 N.Y.S.2d 687 (A.D. 2 Dept. 1983), 469 N.Y.S.2d 65 (Ct. App. 1983).

8. Buchanan and Brock, *Deciding for Others*, 142.

9. Buchanan and Brock, *Deciding for Others*, 142.

10. Buchanan and Brock, *Deciding for Others*, 143.

11. Buchanan and Brock, *Deciding for Others*, 236.

12. Buchanan and Brock, *Deciding for Others*, 235.

13. Buchanan and Brock do not define self-regarding or other-regarding interests. They cite Feinberg, who defines other-regarding interests as interests which directly promote the well-being of another for the sake of the other. This contrasts with self-regarding interests in which the concern is with either one's own well-being, or the well-being of others to the extent that they promote one's own well-being. See J. Feinberg, *The Moral Limits of the Criminal Law: i: Harm to Others* (New York: Oxford University Press, 1984), 74–5.

14. Buchanan and Brock, *Deciding for Others*, 133.

15. Buchanan and Brock, *Deciding for Others*, 236.

16. Buchanan and Brock, *Deciding for Others*, 236.

17. Buchanan and Brock, *Deciding for Others*, 123.

18. While it is true that trade-offs are necessary in all groups, what makes such intrafamilial trade-offs unique is that the child whose interest is being compromised is not capable of doing so voluntarily. Instead the child is represented by a guardian (parent) who represents the aforementioned child and other members of the family who will benefit from the child's compromise. Outside of the intimate family, this would not be permitted as the guardian would be said to have a conflict of interest. I discussed in Chapter 2 why I believe that parents are the appropriate guardian despite the potential conflict of interest.

19. F. Schoeman, 'Parental Discretion and Children's Rights: Background and Implications for Medical Decision-Making', *Journal of Medicine and Philosophy*, 10 (February 1985), 48–9.

20. I. Kant, *Grounding for the Metaphysics of Morals* (1785), trans. J. W.

Ellington (Indianapolis, Ind.: Hackett Publishing, 1981), paragraph 429.

21. B. Brody, *Life and Death Decision Making* (New York: Oxford University Press, 1988), 33 (footnote omitted).

22. B. Brody, 'Towards a Theory of Respect for Persons', in O. Green (ed.), *Respect for Persons: Tulane Studies in Philosophy*, 31 (1982), 65.

23. Brody, *Life and Death Decision Making*, 34.

24. What does a feature of proportionate respect mean for those individuals who will never attain the full capacities of personhood (e.g. a child with Down's syndrome)? Brody argues that such individuals are deserving of respect in part because they are members of a class who have the potential to become Kantian persons, and in part because they, themselves, will develop some of the capacities associated with personhood. See Brody, *Life and Death Decision Making*, 34.

    The issues regarding disabled children and the respect that is owed them is a whole separate topic that I do not address in this book. The interested reader should see R. M. Veatch, *The Foundations of Justice: Why the Retarded and the Rest of Us Have Claims to Equality* (New York: Oxford University Press, 1986).

25. That moral behaviour differs between personal and impersonal relationships is widely, although not universally, accepted. Aristotle, for example, discusses the difference between household and public justice. See Aristotle, *Nicomachean Ethics*, book V and *Politics*, books I and III. However, what morality demands in the personal realm has not been fully elaborated upon. Two recent works which explore this issue are G. Graham and H. LaFollette (eds.), *Person to Person* (Philadelphia, Pa.: Temple University Press, 1989), and H. LaFollette, *Personal Relationships: Love, Identity, and Morality* (Cambridge, Mass.: Blackwell Publishers, 1996).

26. My position is in opposition to J. Feinberg, 'The Child's Right to an Open Future', in W. Aiken and H. LaFollette (eds.), *Whose Child? Children's Rights, Parental Authority, and State Power* (Totowa, NJ: Littlefield, Adams, 1980), 124–53.

27. Wisconsin v. Yoder, 406 U.S. 205 (1972), Justice White concurring, joined by Justices Brennan and Stewart, as quoted in R. H. Mnookin and D. K. Weisberg (eds.), *Child, Family and State: Problems and Materials on Children and the Law*, 2nd ed. (Boston, Mass.: Little, Brown, 1989), 61 (emphasis added).

28. M. Walzer, *Spheres of Justice: A Defense of Pluralism and Equality* (New York: Basic Books, 1983).

29. Walzer, *Spheres of Justice*, 6–10.

30. If Amy were being medically neglected, then her parents' decision

would be contrary to the negative component of the modified principle of respect. This would create the need for intervention.

31. Again, I believe, but do not argue, that parents can choose to sacrifice their own basic needs. For the purpose of this book, I am only interested in whether a surrogate decision maker, in particular, a parent, can compromise the interests of her dependent. I argue that she can, but that she cannot choose to sacrifice any of the basic needs of her child.

32. The modified principle of respect is an appropriate guidance principle for parents in intimate families. When families are not intimate, the intrafamilial trade-offs permitted by this guidance principle may place the child in serious danger. Even if it does not, wide parental autonomy and strict restrictions on intervention cannot be justified. In an intimate family, wide parental autonomy allows parents to promote common goods even when it requires some compromise of the child's own particular interests. In a non-intimate family, such autonomy shields the parents from appropriate scrutiny. While privacy is necessary to promote and respect intimacy, privacy without intimacy places the already vulnerable child in a more vulnerable position. In these situations, I would argue that if the child's parents continue to be the surrogate decision makers, then they must be held to a standard which focuses on the child's self-regarding interests. That is, they should be held to a best interest standard such as the one proposed by Buchanan and Brock. In these situations, state intervention should be more liberally permitted.

33. Buchanan and Brock, *Deciding for Others*, 142.

4

Respect for the Competent Child

1. *Two Objections to Constrained Parental Autonomy*

In the development of constrained parental autonomy as a decision-making model for children in intimate families, I made the assumption that all children are incompetent and that parents should be the *sole* decision makers regarding their child's health care decisions. I want to consider two objections which support giving children a greater role in the decision-making process. The first objection is based on competency and its relationship to autonomy in health care decision making. Competent adults have health care decision-making autonomy. If autonomy is based solely on competency, then competent children should also have health care decision-making autonomy.[1] I will argue that competency is a necessary but not a sufficient condition for respecting a child's health care decision-making autonomy.

The second objection is popular among child liberationists, who seek to grant children equal rights with their adult counterparts. They argue that justice demands that we treat equal persons equally and that differences between children and adults are not morally relevant. The objection can take one of two forms. Some liberationists seek to lower the age of health care decision-making autonomy by lowering the age of consent. To a large extent, their theories are based on the presumption that competency should entail respect for autonomy. Other liberationists, however, seek to emancipate children of all ages, even though the youngest may be unable to use their rights effectively.

Although I reject both liberationist positions, I do not claim that children, particularly competent children, should be ignored in the decision-making process. Rather, in the fifth section of this chapter, I reconsider the principle of respect for persons, modified to apply to children as a constraint on parental autonomy. I argue that it supports a role for children which depends on the child's competency, the type of decision, and the context in which the decision is being made.

2. *The Competency Argument: Empirical Data*

What does it meant to call someone competent? In health care, competency is generally agreed to be a decision-specific, context-relative property, and not a global, all-or-nothing property.[2] To call someone competent is to say that the person is capable of making a voluntary health care decision that promotes her own conception of the good. In general, adults are presumed competent on the basis of age, and physicians are not allowed to perform any medical procedure without the patient's 'informed consent'. In contrast, non-emancipated children are presumed incompetent and their parents have surrogate decision-making authority.

An adult's health care decisions are respected because it is presumed that he is competent to make such decisions. It is not enough for the physician to disagree with the patient's plan of action, or for the physician to believe that the patient's plan is not in the patient's best interest. Rather, the physician should question only the process by which the person makes a decision rather than the actual content of the decision.[3]

The presumption of adult competency is overinclusive. There are many adults who are not capable of synthesizing risks, benefits, and alternatives, and then making a decision based on that information. Likewise, the presumption of child incompetence is overinclusive. A young child may be unable to make a competent decision as to whether she needs a vaccination, but she may be competent to decide in which arm she wants the injection. An adolescent may be competent to decide between various potential treatments for an infected toe, but may be unable to fully synthesize the pros and cons of two different cancer regimens. Or an adolescent may be competent to decide between two treatments proposed hypothetically, but may be unable to make such a decision in an actual clinical setting. Competency is relative to the individual's cognitive development, the type of decision, and the context in which the decision is made. I address the relationship between competency and autonomy in section 3 below. Here I want to focus on the concept of informed consent.

The legal doctrine of informed consent enables a competent adult patient to express his autonomy in health care decision making. The process of informed consent consists of two separate legal duties. First, it is the physician's duty to disclose the medical findings to the patient in language which he can understand. The physician must explain the prognosis, the proposed treatment and its alternatives, and the risks and benefits of the various treatments, including the option of refusing treatment. The patient is free to ask questions and to have facts repeated to aid understanding. He may also consult with other health care providers and discuss the options with his family. Second, it is the duty of the physician to obtain the patient's consent or refusal. If he consents, the physician may administer treatment. If he refuses, the physician must respect the patient's wishes; to do otherwise would be assault and battery.

There are serious problems with information disclosure by physicians who tend to minimize uncertainty and gloss over many risks.[4] My focus, however, is on the second duty, and what it means for the patient to give consent. This can be divided into three components: that the patient's consent is informed (made knowingly), is competent (made intelligently), and is voluntary.[5] A survey of the literature reveals scant empirical data. Those which exist suggest that most health care decisions made by adults and children do not fulfil the three components listed above. The data also suggest that adults and older children do not significantly differ in their consent skills.[6]

Can a patient act knowingly? To act knowingly in the consent process is to 'understand the consensual meanings of the words and phrases of the message'.[7] In a review of the literature, Thomas Grisso and Linda Vierling concluded that '[w]e have practically no systematic information regarding children's understanding of the meanings of terms that are likely to arise in situations in which consent to therapy is sought'.[8] Nor do the data show that adults are capable of acting knowingly. Paul Appelbaum, Charles Lidz, and Alan Meisel cite empirical studies which suggest that many adults 'frequently fail to understand the information they are told or expected to read'.[9] The failure can be due to inadequate cognitive and intellectual capacities or to the clinical and affective context in which the information is given.

Whether patients can make a competent decision depends upon whether they can understand the treatment alternatives and the consequences of each decision. In general, children's understanding parallels their general cognitive development. Using the stages characterized by Piaget,[10] children between the ages of two and seven are 'preoperational', a stage in which they 'can see only one aspect of a phenomenon at a time, find no conflict in circular reasoning, and cannot generalize from one experience or observation to another similar one'.[11] Around age seven, children reach the stage of 'concrete operational' thought, which is less egocentric and employs some elementary logic. Around puberty, children move into the stage of 'formal operational' thought, in which they begin to think abstractly, imagine alternatives, and begin to consider the possible long-term and short-term consequences of their decisions. However, Ellen Perrin and Susan Gerrity found that only one-third of the eighth-graders (thirteen- and fourteen-year-olds) had reached the Piagetian stage of formal operations, which is indicative of their ability to make a competent decision.[12]

Although one might intuit that the biggest difference between children and adult decision making would be in this component of informed consent, the empirical data are insufficient to test whether consent given by adults is significantly different (presumably better) than consent given by competent children. The few studies that do compare adolescent and adult decision making have not shown marked differences in process or content.[13] For example, Lois Weithorn and Susan Campbell asked subjects of four different ages (nine, fourteen, eighteen, and twenty-one) to answer questions regarding four hypothetical medical dilemmas. The authors found that 'the performance of the fourteen-year-olds was *generally* equivalent to that of the adults', but that nine-year-olds were notably less able to understand the medical information.[14]

Whether the patient makes a voluntary decision is related to whether the patient can knowingly and intelligently come to a rational decision and act on this decision, or whether the patient acquiesces to others. To be voluntary, a decision must be purposeful, intentional, and free from compulsion and coercion.[15] Like competency, it is more accurate to consider voluntariness as a matter of degree and not as an all-or-nothing property. While susceptibility to authority and conformity to peers undermine voluntariness, whether a decision made under such influences is voluntary depends on the degree to which the susceptibility influences the decision-making process.

The data suggest that early adolescents are highly submissive to authority and are likely to conform to social norms and expectations. Peer conformity tends to diminish by mid-adolescence, and by age fifteen the risk of deferent response has significantly diminished,[16] although parental influence remains strong. One study of forty fourteen- and fifteen-year-old subjects demonstrated that adolescents tended to defer to their parents on most issues, particularly as parental influence became more demanding.[17] However, the scant data reveal that adults are also prone to defer to authority,[18] and that they tend to conform to peers.[19]

Despite the data, David Scherer and N. Dickon Reppucci claim that most of the studies do not reflect what actually occurs because the studies depict hypothetical situations which may not accurately capture the differences that would be revealed in 'a more naturalistic setting'.[20] For example, it is not known whether the stress of illness has the same influence on the decision-making capabilities of adolescents and adults. William Gardner, David Scherer, and Maya Tester believe that the impact of stress would be more harmful to the decisions of adolescents than to the decisions of adults although they cite no data on which to base their belief.[21]

Overall, the empirical data regarding competency of children as compared to adults are insufficient. Nevertheless, they do suggest that by age twelve, fourteen, or sixteen (depending on the study and theory), there may not be a clear rationale to characterize children *as a class* as incompetent or as incapable of giving informed consent. While the intellectual capacity and competency of adolescents to provide informed consent span a wide spectrum, the same is true of a random sample of adults.[22] Yet adults are presumed to be competent and are empowered to give informed consent unless they are shown to be incompetent; children are presumed to be incompetent and require surrogate decision makers (in general, their parents). If competency is the only criterion on which respect for autonomy in health care is based, this difference cannot be justified.

3. *Autonomy Reconsidered*

Given that competency is context-specific, it is not surprising that there is no test which can easily distinguish between a competent and an incompetent individual. Even if an objective test could be devised, individual tests of competency of every potential patient would exact a high price in terms of efficiency, privacy, and respect for autonomy. Instead, respect for autonomy in health care is based not only on competency but also on age.[23]

To some extent the age standard is arbitrary, as there are individuals older than the legal age of emancipation who are incompetent and individuals younger than the legal age of emancipation who are competent. But the statutes are not capricious; in general, individuals above the legal age are more likely to be competent than individuals below the legal age.[24] I need to demonstrate that even if a child is competent, there are advantages in treating her differently from an adult, particularly with regard to respect for her autonomy.

One moral argument to limit the child's short-term freedom is based on the argument that parents and other authorities need to promote the child's long-term autonomy. Given the value that is placed on self-determination, it makes sense to grant adults autonomy, provided they have some threshold level of competency. Respect is shown by respecting their present project pursuits.[25] But respect for a threshold of competency in children places the emphasis on short-term autonomy rather than on a child's lifetime autonomy. Children need a protected period in which to develop 'enabling virtues' (habits, including the habit of self-control), which advance their lifetime autonomy and opportunities.[26] Although many adults would also benefit from the development of their potential and the improvement of their skills and self-control, at some point (and it is reasonable to use the age of emancipation as the proper cut-off), the advantages of self-determination outweigh the benefits of further guidance and its potential to improve long-term autonomy.

A related argument to limit the child's short-term freedom is that the child's decisions are based on limited experience, so that his decisions are not part of a well-conceived life plan. Although there are many adults with limited experience, children have a greater potential for the improvement of their knowledge base and their skills of critical reflection and self-control.[27] As Willard Gaylin explains: 'Surely, part of what goes into our abridgement of the child's autonomy is the recognition that although he may be [competent] . . . the limitations of his experience distorts his capacity for sound judgement.'[28] By protecting the child from his own impetuosity, his parents help him obtain the background knowledge and the capacities that will allow him to make decisions that better promote his life plans. His parents' attempt to help him flourish may not be achieved, but that does not invalidate the attempt.

A third moral argument why childhood competency should not entail respect for the child's autonomy depends upon the significant role that intimate families play in our lives. In general, family autonomy promotes the interests and goals of both the children and the parents. It serves the needs and interests of the child to have autonomous parents who will help her become an autonomous individual capable of devising and implementing her own life plan. It serves the adults interest in having and raising a family according to their own vision of the good life.[29] These interests do not abruptly cease when the child becomes competent. If anything, parents then have the opportunity to inculcate their beliefs through rational discourse, instead of through example, bribery, or force.[30]

If family intimacy is valuable both for what it does and for what it is, then family autonomy should not terminate the moment that a child attains some threshold level of competency. Rather, families can continue to pursue family goals which may compete with the individual goals of family members, even of competent family members. As the ultimate arbiters of intrafamilial conflicts, parents have the right and responsibility to choose these goals. This is not to suggest that parents should not give their child's opinions serious consideration, particularly if the child is competent; only that parents should retain final decision-making authority until the age of emancipation.[31] Although the child's present-day autonomy is overridden, respect for family autonomy serves to promote the direction and development of the child's lifetime autonomy. As such, respect for family autonomy respects the child's developing personhood.

There are also pragmatic reasons to justify overriding the present-day autonomy of competent children. First, although it may be desirable to obtain a determination of competency for unusually mature and competent children, no such test exists. Second, it may be best if parents recognize their children's maturity and treated them accordingly, but deny that this justifies granting competent children legal emancipation. Many parents respect their mature child's decisions voluntarily, and '[i]t is plausible to think that children's maturity is not completely unrelated to parental good sense'. [32] Although child liberationists may object because a voluntary approach only encourages but does not legally enforce respect for the adolescent's autonomy, such an approach does limit the state's role in intrafamilial decisions which is important for the family's ability to flourish. [33]

In summary, I believe that adults should be presumed competent and their autonomy should be respected unless they are proven incompetent. There are morally relevant differences between competent children and adults which justify different treatment with respect to autonomy. A competent child's short-term autonomy can be morally overridden to promote his lifetime autonomy because of his potential to improve his decision-making skills and to broaden his background knowledge, and because of his parents' valid interest and responsibility in supporting and guiding his moral and cognitive development, even if he has achieved a threshold level of competency.

4. *Liberationist Arguments*

Child liberationists support granting children equal rights; they are popular in both academic circles[34] and the White House.[35] They argue that children are the last oppressed group in society and lament that child protection and not child liberation remains the legal ideal. They argue that children should have equal rights with their adult counterparts. However, the rights that adults need to flourish are not the same as those needed by children. In general, adults need mostly negative rights (e.g. the rights of non-interference and self-determination). Children also need negative rights (e.g. the right not to be physically, sexually, or emotionally abused), but they also need a wide variety of positive rights (e.g. the rights to an education, adequate nutrition, and medical care). Child protectionists justify the difference on the grounds that children are less powerful, more vulnerable, and more needy of protection. Child liberationists claim that such treatment further increases their powerlessness and vulnerability.

Child liberationists can be classified into two groups, depending on when they believe that children should be emancipated. The more conservative liberationists seek to redraw the line for emancipation based on competency or rationality. They do not deny that young children need surrogate decision makers, but they believe that by mid- to late adolescence, children are competent and that their autonomy in health care and other spheres of decision making should be respected. Their position can be refuted by the arguments from the previous section which found that competency is a necessary but not a sufficient condition for respecting a child's autonomy.

The more radical liberationists, on the other hand, endorse equal rights for all children regardless of their capacities. This does not mean that 'children would be emancipated, not forced to go to school, permitted to vote and to work, etc. and that all else would remain the same'.[36] Rather, it is a radical proposal with wide repercussions. Richard Farson, for example, enumerates some of the freedoms which it would imply: the right to self-determination, the right to alternate home environments, the right to information, the right to educate oneself, the right to freedom from physical punishment, the right to sexual freedom, the right to economic power, and the right to justice in the legal system.[37]

Several liberationists have offered book-length accounts of what it would mean for children to have equal rights with adults.[38] In order for these theories to have any force, there needs to be a mechanism which enables children to exercise these rights, regardless of their capacities. One proposal is to create a class of agents who help children exercise their rights.[39] In proposing the idea of child agents, Howard Cohen explains that 'borrowing the capacities of others is not at all unusual; we all do it at one time or another'.[40] Cohen uses the examples of the adult who hires a lawyer to draw up his will or a physician to suture his laceration.

Cohen's proposal to implement children's rights is incomplete and self-contradictory. He specifically denies that parents should serve as their child's agents because of the potential conflicts of interest.[41] Cohen also rejects the idea of a professional class of child agents with licensing requirements because that might limit the number of agents and make their services too scarce. He argues that the agents should not be paid because this might discriminate against children who could not afford to retain them.[42] There is no way that child agents can be made accountable if there are no standards; nor can a child who is incapable of asserting his or her own rights choose an agent or evaluate the agent's work. And who will be willing to learn the skills necessary to become a child agent and exert long hours for no remuneration, particularly when the child can unilaterally choose to dissolve the relationship at any time? The role of child agents seems to offer adults all the responsibilities of parenthood without most of its potential rewards.

I reject the child liberationist's goal to grant children equal rights with adults. Children have and need rights, even if they are not the same as those held by adults. To empower children with the same rights as adults is to deny them the protection they need. It would mean the dissolution of child labour laws, mandatory education, statutory rape laws, and child neglect statutes. It would leave children even more vulnerable than they presently are.

The child liberationist movement denies internal value to the intimate family. The family is judged purely on the basis of its utility and popularity. Cohen, for example, argues that a child should be allowed to change families, either because the child's parents are abusive, or because a neighbour or wealthy stranger offers him a better deal.[43] This ignores the important role that continuity and permanence play in the parent–child relationship,[44] traits the child may not yet appreciate.

Respect for an individual's autonomy means respecting both her good and bad decisions. Child liberation requires respect for a child's present-day freedom regardless of its long-term impact on her developing personhood. Imagine, then, that a fourteen-year-old adolescent with new-onset diabetes refuses to take insulin because of a fear of needles (or because her boyfriend's religious beliefs proscribe medical care) even though she understands that she will die without it. Who is willing to abandon her to her autonomy?

The liberationist may object because adults also make bad decisions. But the inadequacy of some adults (or some of their decisions) is not the standard on which respect for autonomy is or should be based. Purdy also rejects the least-common-denominator approach:

Even liberationists, after all, lament the mistakes and immorality of adults. It seems to be that instead of asserting children's rights to be equally silly and weak, it would be at least plausible to argue for the overriding importance of helping children develop the self-control and other enabling virtues necessary for living more satisfying and moral lives.[45]

Although physicians ought to challenge adults whom they perceive to be making bad decisions, ultimately the competent adult's decision prevails. Respect for autonomy means respect for a person's good and bad decisions. I am unwilling, however, to respect the fourteen-year-old diabetic child's refusal of treatment or to respect a competent child's present-day autonomy whenever she makes a bad decision. But if I am unwilling to respect her autonomy on the basis of content, then I am not respecting her autonomy. To respect only those decisions that a child makes with which I (or her own physician) agree does not show respect for the child's autonomy, but makes a farce out of what is meant by respect for autonomy.[46]

5. *The Model of Constrained Parental Autonomy Revisited*

In Chapter 3, I argued that parents should be the decision makers for their children, but that parental autonomy should not be absolute. Rather, parental autonomy should be constrained by a principle of respect for persons that is modified to apply to children. I assumed that children were incompetent and should not have health care autonomy. In this chapter, I have argued that we should respect parental autonomy even after a child has developed some threshold level of competence, because competency is a necessary but not a sufficient condition to require respect for a child's health care autonomy.

   If denial of a child's autonomy is always consistent with the modified principle of respect, then parental decision making *alone* is the appropriate source of *all* decisions for both competent and incompetent children, and the parents' decision should *always* be respected. However, if there are cases in which the denial of a competent child's dissent does not respect the child's developing and partially actualized personhood, then the competent child's consent is necessary and his dissent must be binding.[47]

Consider two hypothetical cases. In case 1, a sixteen-year-old adolescent needs a blood count for his camp physical. The physician who is about to obtain the blood asks whether she can draw an extra teaspoon for experimental purposes. The physician explains that the experiment will not directly benefit the child or his family, but it also entails minimal, if any additional risk, harm, or inconvenience. The parents consent, the child objects.[48]

In case 2, a thirteen-year-old child has chronic renal failure and will die in several weeks without a transplant. Her sixteen-year-old sister is the only good match. The transplant team explains to the potential donor and her parents that the donation has some significant risks and that it will require the donor to miss six weeks of school. The parents consent to the harvest; the potential child donor objects.[49]

In each case, there are two relationships to be examined: the relationship of the physician to the child patient and his or her family, and the relationship of the child to his or her family. For the purpose of this chapter, I will only examine what respect requires in the latter relationship. The questions I want to address are: (1) Can parental authorization over the competent child's objection be respectful of the child's developing personhood? and (2) Are there cases in which the competent child's consent is necessary to be respectful of his or her developing personhood?

Can authorization over the competent child's dissent ever be respectful of the child's developing and partially actualized personhood? Generally, I believe parents do themselves and their children a big disservice if they fail to include their children in the decision-making process. To include the child serves both instrumental and intrinsic purposes. It allows the child to observe firsthand how persons whom she respects and admires make health care decisions. It helps the health care providers and her parents gain her cooperation, which may be necessary to maximize the benefits of the procedure. Her inclusion may also avoid the negative repercussions that her exclusion may create, particularly when the procedure does not benefit her directly. In addition, the child's participation in the decision-making process lets the child know that her parents and her physician respect her and her developing decision-making skills.

In the first case, the parents' decision to permit the physician to procure an extra blood sample entails no additional pain, risk, or harm. Parents frequently authorize their child to do many activities which entail greater risks, harms, and inconvenience (e.g. baby-sitting for a sibling, running an errand). This authority is necessary for the emotional and moral development of the child and for the functioning of the family free from third-party scrutiny. If the child dissents, his parents and physicians should seek to understand his reasons. An explanation of the value of the research and why his blood sample is valuable may teach him an important lesson about science, research, community goals, social obligations, and moral and familial values. As a result of the explanation, the competent child may consent. If not, his parents can still choose to authorize the extra sample. Parents have both the privilege and the responsibility of shaping their child according to their own conception of the good. Parental authorization of their child's participation in minimal-risk research (i.e. research which does not threaten the child's basic needs) over the competent child's dissent is *consistent* with parental autonomy constrained by a modified principle of respect. As such, parents morally can authorize their child's participation, although it is also moral for them to respect their child's dissent.

In the second case, the child's participation as a kidney donor entails risks and harm that are more than a minor increase over minimal risk. The donation threatens her long-term autonomy. If the potential child donor sees the well-being of intimate family members as an integral part of her life plans, then the donation will promote her life plans even while it risks the course that her life plans will follow. Competent individuals accept risks, particularly when they perceive the benefits to significantly out-weigh the possible costs. That is why some competent individuals elect to drive, to ski, and to drink alcohol. If, on the other hand, the competent child does not value the well-being of her sibling or her family, then the potential serious threat to her own well-being threatens to sacrifice her basic needs. Her forced participation would be contrary to her developing and partially actualized personhood.

If a competent child gives informed consent to the donation, it means that the donation serves her interests. Parents still have ultimate responsibility (morally, financially, and legally) to protect their child from harm, and so they must also consent to their child's participation. That is, both the child's and the parents' consent are necessary to ensure that the competent child's participation is respectful of her developing and partially actualized personhood.

Whereas parental consent was necessary and sufficient in case 1, it is necessary but not sufficient in case 2. As the severity or likelihood of risks and harms increases, the threat to the child's basic needs increases. The child's consent does not negate the threat, but competent individuals are allowed to accept such risks. However, the child's informed refusal makes her participation contrary to her basic needs, *both* present and future. As such, her participation over her refusal is *not* consistent with respect for her developing and partially actualized personhood. Thus, parental autonomy constrained by the modified principle of respect permits parents to authorize their child's participation in case 1 regardless of the competent child's own position, but requires both the parents' and the child's consent in case 2. The modified principle of respect accommodates wide parental autonomy in making decisions for their children, even their competent children, but this autonomy is not absolute. As case 2 demonstrates, sometimes the competent child's consent is necessary and must be binding.

The two cases serve to show the flexibility of the model of constrained parental autonomy as a decision-making model. The purpose of the second half of this book is to show how this model is applied in a wide variety of health care situations. There may be cases in which some readers believe that respect for the child's developing personhood should require that the child's consent is binding, whereas other readers may support the parents' right to override the child's dissent. Given the presumption of parental autonomy, I support the parents' decision in cases in which both decisions are consistent with respect for the child's developing personhood. The result is that my interpretation may permit wider parental autonomy than some readers would prefer.

Notes

1. To call someone competent for health care decisions is too broad, as it requires that the individual be competent for all therapeutic health care decisions, which include life-threatening as well as less critical illnesses, and that the individual be competent to make non-therapeutic decisions, such as whether to serve as an organ donor or as a subject of human experimentation. The ability to make competent decisions may vary depending on the situation. I will consider some of these differences in the second half of this book when I consider the application of my model to these different spheres of health care decision making. For now, unless I specify otherwise, I will assume that the decision to be made is for an acute but non-life-threatening medical problem.

2. See, for example, The President's Commission for the Study of Ethical Problems in Medicine and Biomedical and Behavioral Research, *Making Health Care Decisions: The Ethical and Legal Implications of Informed Consent in the Patient–Practitioner relationship*, i (Washington, DC: U.S. Government Printing Office, 1982); and P. S. Appelbaum, C. W. Lidz, and A. Meisel, *Informed Consent: Legal Theory and Clinical Practice* (New York: Oxford University Press, 1987), Chap. 5: 'Exceptions to the Legal Requirements: Incompetency', esp. 5.1 and 5.2.

   In contrast, Abernethy holds the dissenting position that competency is a more general property. See V. Abernethy, 'Compassion, Control, and Decisions About Competency', *American Journal of Psychiatry*, 141 (1984), 53–60.

3. Dave Schmidtz correctly points out that this is what ought to happen, but that in the real world, physicians question both the process and content, particularly when they disagree with the patient's decision. Clinical medical ethicists are trying to change this practice.

4. J. Katz, 'Why Doctors Don't Disclose Uncertainty', *Hastings Center Report*, 14 (1984), 35–44.

5. T. Grisso and L. Vierling, 'Minor's Consent to Treatment: A Developmental Perspective', *Professional Psychology*, 9 (1978), 415.

6. Grisso and Vierling, 'Minor's Consent'.

7. Grisso and Vierling, 'Minor's Consent', 416.

8. Grisso and Vierling, 'Minor's Consent', 417.

9. Appelbaum, Lidz, and Meisel, *Informed Consent*, 57. See their references in Chap. 7, 146–8.

10. J. Piaget, *The Child's Conception of Physical Causality* (Patterson, NJ: Littlefield, Adams, 1960).

11. E. C. Perrin and P. S. Gerrity, 'There's a Demon in Your Belly: Children's Understanding of Illness', *Pediatrics*, 67 (1981), 842.

12. Perrin and Gerrity, 'There's a Demon', 847. Of note, a significant number of adults may never reach the formal operation stage, and yet they are presumed competent to give informed consent.
13. W. Gardner, D. Scherer, and M. Tester, 'Asserting Scientific Authority: Cognitive Development and Adolescent Legal Right.', *American Psychologist*, 44 (1989), 897–9. The authors cite many of the studies that do exist.
14. L. Weithorn and S. Campbell, 'The Competency of Children and Adolescents to Make Informed Treatment Decisions', *Child Development*, 53 (1982), 1595 (emphasis added). I italicized the word 'generally' because the fourteen-year-olds did reject appropriate anti-seizure medicine more often than adults, which Weithorn and Campbell suggested was consistent with the literature in which adolescents show greater concern for body image (Weithorn and Campbell, 'The Competency', 1596, includes citations to the literature). In their study, the treatment was described as possibly causing periodontal problems and hirsutism (excess growth of body hair). The psychologists concluded, 'These differences do suggest that competency, as defined by certain legal tests, may depend to some degree upon the dimension of the specific decision making context.' Weithorn and Campbell, 'The Competency', 1596.

    Noteworthy is that despite the difficulty in comprehension, the preferences of the nine-year-old subjects did not differ significantly from the preferences expressed by their adolescent and adult counterparts regarding treatment. See Weithorn and Campbell, 'The Competency', 1596.
15. D. G. Scherer and N. D. Reppucci, 'Adolescents' Capacities to Provide Voluntary Informed Consent', *Law and Human Behavior*, 12 (1988), 124.
16. Numerous studies are cited by Grisso and Vierling, 'A Minor's Consent', 421–2. Some of these same studies are cited by Scherer and Reppucci, 'Adolescents' Capacities', 125.
17. Scherer and Reppucci, 'Adolescents' Capacities', 123–41. Scherer and Reppucci considered five hypothetical cases, four of which were therapeutic (tonsillitis, depression, enuresis, and warts), and one of which was non-therapeutic (organ donation). Their data revealed greater deference to parents in the first four cases as compared to the latter. Scherer and Reppucci concluded that their data supported the claim that adolescents were less deferential 'when the consequences or gravity of the decision has serious implications for the adolescent's health' (Scherer and Reppucci, 'Adolescents' Capacities', 136). The problem is that the adolescents may have been less deferential because the donation did not promote their own medical well-being

in contrast with the other scenarios. Further study would need to be done to determine whether adolescents are less deferential in non-therapeutic decisions in general, or whether they are less deferential in decisions which entail significant risk to the adolescent's health. The present data do not support the conclusion that adolescents are less deferential on all medical issues of a serious nature.

18. The classic study was performed by Milgram in the 1960s. In Milgram's study, a large percentage of adults complied with authority figures when they were told to shock innocent subjects with volts of electricity large enough to be fatal. See S. Milgram, *Obedience to Authority: An Experimental View* (New York: Harper and Row, 1974).

19. S. E. Asch, 'Effects of Group Pressure Upon the Modification and Distortion of Judgements', in H. Guetzkow (ed.), for the U.S. Office of Naval Research, *Groups, Leadership and Men: Research in Human Relations* (Pittsburgh, Pa.: Carnegie Press, 1951), 177–90.

20. Scherer and Reppucci, 'Adolescents' Capacities', 133.

21. Gardner, Scherer, and Tester, 'Asserting Scientific Authority', 899–900.

22. C. Tomlinson-Keasey, 'Formal Operations in Females from Eleven to Fifty-Four Years of Age', *Developmental Psychology*, 6 (1972), 364, as cited by Grisso and Vierling, 'Minor's Consent', 421.

23. The presumption of childhood incompetency is being curtailed in the United States by state policies that recognize 'mature minors' and 'emancipated minors', as well as by the specialized consent statutes. In most cases, I believe that we are doing children a disservice when we abandon them to their autonomy.

A similar movement is occurring in Great Britain. Although the legal age of health care decisions is sixteen (Family Law Reform Act, 1969), in contrast with eighteen in the United States, the *Gillick* case encouraged physicians to respect the consent of minors younger than sixteen on a case-by-case judgement of competency (*Gillick v. W Norfolk & Wisbech HA* [1985] 3 All ER 402). However, several more recent cases substantially limit this ruling. See, *Re R* [1991] 4 All ER 177; *Re W* [1992] 4 All ER 627; *Re E* [1993] 1 FLR 1065; and *Re S* [1994] 2 FLR 1065.

24. The specific age at which emancipation should be granted is a political and not a moral question. Any age cut-off will liberate some immature individuals and will delay the liberation of some mature children. I do not argue for any particular age because I believe that the age should be chosen by societal consensus, and may differ in different cultures and different eras.

25. The notion of rational beings as project pursuers is explored in detail by B. Williams, 'Utilitarianism and Integrity', in J. Perry and M.

Bratman (eds.), *Introduction of Philosophy: Classical and Contemporary Readings*, 2nd ed. (New York: Oxford University Press, 1993), 558–66; and L. E. Lomasky, *Persons, Rights and the Moral Community* (New York: Oxford University Press, 1987).

26. L. M. Purdy, *In Their Best Interest? The Case Against Equal Rights for Children* (New York: Cornell University Press, 1992), 45.

27. Purdy, *In Their Best Interest*, 76–84.

28. W. Gaylin, 'Competence: No Longer All or None', in W. Gaylin and R. Macklin (eds.), *Who Speaks for the Child: The Problems of Proxy Consent* (New York: Plenum Press, 1982), 35.

29. Of course, the parents themselves may disagree on goals, values, and what the good life entails. Parents in an intimate relationship generally can reach agreement in a way that does not violate the respect that they owe each other. I discuss this briefly in Chapter 6.3.

30. Gaylin makes a similar argument. See Gaylin, 'Competence: No Longer', 31.

31. Gaylin reaches the same conclusion. See Gaylin, 'Competence: No Longer', 47–8.

32. See, Purdy, *In Their Best Interest*, 78. And in fact, Norwegian research with ten- to twelve-year-olds suggests that children's competence follows adults' expectations. See A. Solberg, 'Negotiating Childhood: Changing Constructions of Age for Norwegian Children', in A. James and A. Prout (eds.), *Constructing and Reconstructing Childhood: New Directions in the Sociological Study of Childhood* (London: Falmer Press, 1990), 118–37.

33. Gaylin makes a similar argument in 'Competence: No Longer', 47–8.

34. See, for example, H. Cohen, *Equal Rights for Children* (Totowa, NJ: Littlefield, Adams, 1980); and J. Harris, 'The Political Status of Children', in K. Graham (ed.), *Contemporary Political Philosophy* (New York: Cambridge University Press, 1982), 35–55.

35. See, for example, H. Rodham, 'Children Under the Law', *Harvard Educational Review*, 43 (1973), 487–514; and H. Rodham, 'Children's Rights: A Legal Perspective', in P. A. Vardin and I. N. Brody (eds.), *Children's Rights: Contemporary Perspectives* (New York: Teachers College Press, 1979), 21–36.

36. Harris, 'Political Status', 50.

37. R. Farson, 'A Child's Bill of Rights', in J. Feinberg and H. Gross (eds.), *Justice: Selected Readings* (Belmont, Calif.: Dickenson Publishing, 1977), 325–8.

38. J. Holt, *Escape from Childhood* (New York: E. P. Dutton, 1974); and Cohen, *Equal Rights*.

39. Cohen, *Equal Rights*, Chap. 6, 'Child Agents'.

40. Cohen, *Equal Rights*, 57.

41. Cohen, *Equal Rights*, 79.
42. Cohen, *Equal Rights*, 86.
43. Cohen, *Equal Rights*, 66.
44. J. Goldstein, A. Freud, and A. J. Solnit, *Before the Best Interests of the Child* (New York: Free Press, 1979), Chap. 1, esp. 199–202, note 10. Cohen specifically rejects the theories of Goldstein, Freud, and Solnit. (Cohen, *Equal Rights*, 66.)
45. Purdy, *In Their Best Interest*, 78.
46. Alderson, one of the most ardent supporters of granting children health care autonomy, limits the health care autonomy of children to those situations where an immediate decision is not necessary and where the decision will not result in irreparable harm. See P. Alderson and J. Montgomery, *Health Care Choices: Making Decisions with Children* (London: Institute for Public Policy Research, 1996). Such limits misconstrue what it means to respect autonomy: '[T]aking freedom seriously means acknowledging the rights of competent individuals to dispose of their lives in ways that others may judge imprudent.' H. T. Engelhardt, Jr., 'Freedom vs. Best Interest: A Conflict at the Roots of Health Care', in L. D. Kliever (ed.), *Dax's Case: Essays in Medical Ethics and Human Meaning* (Dallas, Tex.: Southern Methodist University Press, 1988), 79.
47. In Chapter 5, I consider the possibility that there are some cases in which an incompetent child's assent or dissent should be determinative as well. In Chapter 8, I address the question of whether the child's consent for health care is ever sufficient; that is, whether there are cases in which the child's consent *alone* without concomitant parental permission (or notification) is or ought to be binding. I argue that the child's consent should not be sufficient.
48. This case will be classified in Chapter 5.5 as research that entails at most minimal risks and harms.
49. This case is an example of the child as organ donor, which entails more than a minor increase over minimal risk. This issue is discussed in further detail in Chapter 6.

PART II

Applications of Constrained Parental Autonomy

5

The Child as Research Subject

1. Proxy Consent

The Nuremberg Code was adopted in 1946 in response to the documented abuse of human beings as research subjects by the Nazis. The Code was quite explicit that '[t]he voluntary consent of the human subject is absolutely essential'.[1] There was no mention of proxy consent; the subject had to be able to consent to participation. Later codes of ethics included the possibility of participation by incompetent subjects by permitting proxy consent.[2] Whether such consent is morally adequate, particularly when the incompetent subjects are children, was the topic of a series of articles between two American Christian theologians, Paul Ramsey and Richard McCormick, in the early 1970s. Despite contributions by many other ethicists, there remains vigorous disagreement within the medical ethics community as to the morality of a child's participation as a research subject.

In this chapter, I address the moral question of whether and when children can serve as subjects of human experimentation. My goals are to show that (1) children *can* participate morally as human subjects; (2) the present regulations are overbroad in the scope of research in which children can participate; and (3) the present regulations place too much emphasis on the young child's dissent.

2. Can Children Morally Participate as Human Subjects?

In the early 1970s, Ramsey argued that children should never participate as research subjects in 'non-therapeutic research'[3] (that is, research which offers no direct therapeutic benefit to the children subjects). His first argument is that for research to be moral it requires the informed consent of the subject. Because the child cannot give informed consent, his parents must act as his surrogate. However, parental responsibility to their child is fiduciary, and to authorize their child's participation is a breach of this duty.[4]

McCormick rejected Ramsey's argument, using a natural law approach that states that parental consent 'is morally valid precisely insofar as it is a reasonable presumption of the child's wishes'.[5] McCormick held that there are 'certain identifiable valuables that we *ought* to support, attempt to realize, and never directly suppress because they are definitive of our flourishing and well-being'.[6] The child, then, would want to participate as a research subject because he ought to do so.[7] That is, the child would choose to participate because

[t]o pursue the good that is human life means not only to choose and support this value in one's own case, but also in the case of others when the opportunity arises. In other words, the individual *ought* also to take into account, realize, make efforts in behalf of the lives of others also, for we are social beings and the goods that define our growth and invite to it are goods that reside also in others.[8]

Ramsey rebutted McCormick's argument on the grounds that it was too broad and would justify compulsory altruism.[9] At the extreme, if McCormick's arguments are valid, 'then anyone—and not only children—may legitimately be entered into human experimentation without his will [consent]'.[10]

Ramsey's second argument against using children as research subjects is based on the Kantian principle that persons should never be treated solely as a means, but always simultaneously as an end.[11] Ramsey argued that the use of a child as a research subject in research which offers no direct therapeutic benefit treats the child solely as a means. While it may serve useful societal goals, it fails to serve the child subject's interests and thus cannot be performed morally.

McCormick objected to this argument on the grounds that it presumes an atomistic view of humans. Humans are social beings whose good transcends their individual good. Participation as a research subject is consistent with treating the child as an end understood to mean a social being.[12] The problem with this argument, as McCormick realized, is that it can require the participation of adults in research projects to which they do not give their consent,[13] and while McCormick tolerates this enforced Good Samaritanism, most ethicists and legal scholars do not.

The debate initiated by McCormick and Ramsey continues. The primary consequentialistic motivation for refuting Ramsey's position is that excluding children from research will have long-term negative consequences on the well-being of children in general. Ramsey realized the danger of prohibiting children from participating in all non-therapeutic research because it would leave children 'therapeutic orphans'.[14] His solution was to exhort researchers to 'sin bravely': the trustworthy researcher was the one who did 'not deny the moral force of the imperative he violates'.[15]

Ramsey's arguments are powerful and they remind us of the problems that researchers face when dealing with incompetent subjects. One promising line of argument to justify the participation of children is to refute Ramsey on the grounds that his perspective regarding parental responsibility is too narrow. Henry Beecher argues that parents can authorize a child's participation to promote the child's moral development: 'Parents have the obligation to inculcate into their children attitudes of unselfish service. One could hope that this might be extended to include participation in research for the public welfare, when it is important and there is no discernible risk.'[16]

William Bartholome also argues that parents have the moral authority to permit their children to participate in human experimentation in order to promote their children's moral education.[17] Taking this position further, Terrence Ackerman contends that parents have a *moral duty* to guide the activities of their children because children rely upon adults for guidance. Respect for a child, then, requires that parents 'carefully direct his "choices"'.[18]

Nevertheless, neither Beecher nor Bartholome believed that parental consent was sufficient. Beecher argued for both the child's and the parents' informed consent and given this, only permitted children over the age of fourteen to serve as research subjects.[19] Bartholome took a more liberal view and allowed for the participation of children with their parents' consent if the children could give assent, even if not effective consent.[20] The problem with both of these positions is the practical one that children are usually ill prepared to refuse requests by their physicians and parents.[21]

Ackerman, in contrast, argues that requiring the child's assent makes a mockery both of our duties to children and of their limited present-day capabilities to act autonomously: 'We cannot decide how to intervene in a child's life by projecting what he will come to approve or accept. For what he will come to accept is partly a product of the interventions we make.'[22] Rather, Ackerman argues, parents alone can and must decide whether their children should participate as research subjects.[23]

Although I agree with Ackerman's assessment, he does not offer adequate guidance regarding the limits of parental authority, and whether the child's assent is ever relevant, particularly when the risks are more than minimal. In section 6, I will use the model of constrained parental autonomy to refute Ramsey's arguments. This model will also allow me to formulate guidelines that impose limits on parental autonomy and that delineate the proper role for the child's developing competency and autonomy. These guidelines will be suitably different from those that presently regulate the child's role in human experimentation.

3. *Research Guidelines for Children*

The first guidelines that specifically addressed the role of children in research were produced by the German Ministry of the Interior in 1931.[24] In the United States, recommendations for the participation of children in research were first developed in the 1970s by the National Commission for the Protection of Human Subjects of Biomedical and Behavioral Research.[25] Based on the National Commission's report, the Department of Health, Education, and Welfare (DHEW) circulated preliminary regulations in 1978.[26] In 1983, the newly overhauled Department of Health and Human Services (DHHS) published the revised Federal Regulations regarding the participation of children in human experimentation.[27] In the United Kingdom, in contrast, four distinct guidelines existed regarding the participation of children by 1980.[28] In 1986, the Institute of Medical Ethics working group on the ethics of clinical research investigations proposed new recommendations based on moral theory.[29] Since then, the Medical Research Council and the British Paediatric Association have updated their guidelines.[30] These guidelines are quite similar to (and refer frequently to) the report by the National Commission, unless noted otherwise.

The report by the National Commission begins by justifying its decisions to allow children to participate in human experimentation:

> The Commission recognizes the importance of safeguarding and improving the health and well-being of children, because they deserve the best care that society can reasonably provide. It is necessary to learn more about normal development as well as disease states. . . . Accepted practices must be studied as well, for although infants cannot survive without continual support, the effects of many routine practices are unknown and some have been shown to be harmful.[31]

Although the Commission acknowledged the need to do research on children, it also realized that 'the vulnerability of children, which arises out of their dependence and immaturity raises questions about the ethical acceptability of involving them in research'.[32] To minimize these problems, the Commission established strict criteria that research would need to satisfy. The Commission's report sets them out as follows:

a. The research is scientifically sound and significant;

b. Where appropriate, studies have been conducted first on animals and adult humans, then on older children, prior to involving infants;

c. Risks are minimized by using the safest procedures consistent with sound research design and by using procedures performed for diagnostic or treatment purposes whenever feasible;

d. Adequate provisions are made to protect the privacy of children and their parents and to maintain confidentiality of data;

e. Subjects will be selected in an equitable manner;

f. The conditions of all applicable subsequent conditions are met, and adequate provisions are made for the assent of the child and permission of their parents or guardians.[33]

The Commission recommended additional criteria depending upon the level of risk and harm that the research entailed, the risk/benefit of the proposed project, and the comparative risk/benefit of the alternatives. Local institutional review boards (IRBs) would be created to ensure that these safeguards were fulfilled.[34]

The National Commission classified risk into three categories: minimal risk, a minor increase over minimal risk, and more than a minor increase over minimal risk.[35] The Commission defined minimal risk as 'the probability and magnitude of physical or psychological harm that is normally encountered in the daily lives, or in the routine medical or psychological examination, of healthy children'.[36] The Commission gave several examples including routine immunizations, modest changes in diet or schedule, physical examinations, obtaining blood and urine specimens, and developmental assessments.

When research entails no more than minimal risk, the Commission's recommendations permit the participation of a child as a subject of human experimentation.[37] If the research involves more than minimal risk, the Regulations require the local IRB to determine whether the research presents the prospect of direct therapeutic benefit to the individual patient subject.[38] If the IRB determines that it does, and that the benefits are as favourable to the subjects as those offered by non-experimental alternatives, then the child can serve as a research subject.[39]

However, if the research does not offer the prospect of direct therapeutic benefit, then the IRB can approve the project *only* if the research is likely to yield generalizable knowledge 'of vital importance'.[40] The risks involved in this research may entail only 'a minor increase over minimal risk'.[41] Research that involves greater risk without the prospect of direct benefit (or with the prospect of benefit that is inadequate to justify the risk) may be permitted *only* if it presents 'a reasonable opportunity to further the understanding, prevention, or alleviation of a serious problem affecting the health or welfare of children'.[42] As an additional safeguard, this research requires approval by national review.[43]

Provisions for the solicitation of consent are also under the supervision of the IRBs. For most research, both parental permission and the child's assent are necessary. The Commission explicitly stated that 'assent of the children should be required when

they are seven years of age or older'.[44] The Commission emphasized that the child's dissent should be binding except when
the research offers the potential of direct therapeutic benefit to
the child, in which case the parents can override the child's dissent. The Commission maintained that the decision to override
a child's dissent 'becomes heavier in relation to the maturity of
the particular child'.[45] The Regulations also require that consent
includes parental permission and the child's assent but leave
unspecified the age when assent should be sought. Rather, they
leave it to individual IRBs to take into account 'the age, maturity
and psychological state of the children involved'.[46]

Nevertheless, the National Commission's report and the
Federal Regulations do allow for waivers to the consent process.
For example, parental permission is not necessary if the research
is related to conditions for which adolescents may receive treatment without parental consent,[47] or if the research is designed to
understand and meet the needs of neglected or abused children.[48]
Alternatively, the child's assent is not necessary if the research
offers the prospect of direct therapeutic benefit, and/or if the child
is determined to be unable to give assent (e.g. newborns).

The guidelines of the Federal Regulations are summarized in
table 5.1.

4. Risk

A central feature of the Regulations is the classification of the
research activity according to the degree of risk. As previously
stated, the Commission defines minimal risk as 'the probability
and magnitude of physical or psychological harm that is normally
encountered in the daily lives, or in the routine medical or psychological examination, of healthy children'.[49]

There are several drawbacks to using a standard which comares research activities with typical or routine activities. Ross
hompson argues that a standard based on 'the normative daily
xperiences of children at different ages fails because . . . it potenally permits researchers to act in ways that undermine the child,
ven though these experiences may be familiar to the child'.[50]
hompson argues that children commonly encounter experiences
t school that threaten their self-image, but this does not justify

TABLE 5.1 *Unmodified Classification Scheme of the Federal Regulations on Research Involving Children*

Category of Research	Children Unable to Give Assent	Children Capable of Giving Assent
§ 46.404 research, involving minimal risk	Parental permission alone is necessary and sufficient.	Parental permission is required. Child's dissent is binding.
§ 46.405 research, which offers the prospect of direct therapeutic benefit to the individual subjects. Entails more than minimal risk.	Parental permission alone is necessary and sufficient.	Parental permission alone is necessary and sufficient.
§ 46.406 research, which offers no prospect of direct therapeutic benefit but offers the potential for generalizable knowledge of *vital importance*. Entails no more than a minor increase over minimal risk.	Parental permission alone is necessary and sufficient.	Parental permission is required. Child's dissent is binding.
§ 46.407 research, not otherwise approvable, which presents an opportunity to prevent or alleviate serious health problems of children generally. Entails more than a minor increase over minimal risk.	Subject to national review. Parental permission alone is necessary and sufficient.	Subject to national review. Parental permission is required. Child's dissent is binding.

Source: 48 Fed. Reg. 9814 (1983), at 9818–20.

similar threats in the research setting. Investigators should be hesitant to violate basic ethics principles, although these principles may be regularly violated by others in their everyday life.[51]

The Commission's use of a comparative definition also threatens to increase the vulnerability of children with chronic illnesses, because a child who has been treated for cancer and has received intrathecal medications[52] would find a non-therapeutic lumbar puncture more commensurate with his life experiences than would a healthy child. To use his previous experience to justify additional lumbar punctures for non-therapeutic purposes is highly problematic.[53]

Ackerman suggests that one way to improve the Commission's definition of risk is to understand activities which are 'normally encountered by a child' not to mean any activity which a child may have previously experienced, but rather an activity with which the child is familiar and with which he is able to cope well: 'The fact that a sick child has undergone a particular procedure, such as a lumbar puncture, during treatment does not guarantee that he or she will not be subjected to considerable stress or anxiety.'[54] He has offered the following standard of minimal risk as an alternative: 'A research procedure involving minimal risk is one in which the probability of physical and psychological harm is no more than that to which it is appropriate to intentionally expose a child for educational purposes in family life situations.'[55] I adopt this standard because it allows parents to balance the responsibility of protecting their child from harm and promoting their child's moral development.

The Commission's guidelines are more vague when research involves more than minimal risk. The Commission does not offer a working definition for either 'a minor increase over minimal risk' or 'more than a minor increase over minimal risk'. Rather, it states that in its determination of degree of risk and harm, the IRB should

consider the degree of risk presented by the research from at least the following four perspectives: a common sense estimation of risk, an estimation based upon the investigators' experience with similar interventions or procedures, statistical information that is available regarding such interventions or procedures, and the situation of the proposed subject.[56]

The Commission assumed that there would be agreement within the medical community as to what constitutes different degrees of risk. Jeffery Janofsky and Barbara Starfield distributed a questionnaire to paediatric investigators to assess their perception of the degree of risk associated with a variety of paediatric procedures that are typically used in clinical research, and found few procedures for which there was consensus.[57] Although it had been suggested that the American Academy of Pediatrics create a special task force to develop consensus opinions about the risks of paediatric procedures and interventions to avoid such problems,[58] no such task force was created.

Not only is there disagreement as to which procedures impose what degree of risk, but there are also reasons to suspect that researchers and IRBs underestimate risk. Peter Williams explored three reasons why IRBs tend to underestimate risk.[59] First, most members of an IRB are members of the research community and are inherently biased in support of the value of research and may overestimate the importance of research projects in general. Second, IRBs tend to suffer from group think. Citing James Stoner, Williams explains: '[G]roups confronted with choices involving risks were willing to take more chances than the average of individuals in the groups.'[60]

Third, IRBs have two purposes, which are often in tension: to protect the rights of subjects and to promote their welfare. To respect the subject's right to make an autonomous choice is to allow her to gather all the information regarding a potential trial and decide whether or not to participate. When the subject is a child, her rights are protected by promoting the autonomy of her parents. Institutional protection of the subject's welfare, on the other hand, entails promotion of the subjects' well-being. As such, it might require the universal proscription of certain research projects (e.g. research involving deception), regardless of whether the subject himself or his guardians might consent to participate. Given IRB committee members' own biases in favour of research and self-determination, they tend to do a better job promoting the subjects' right to act autonomously than they do in protecting the subjects' welfare.

Assuming that consensus could be obtained regarding the amount of risk and harm of different procedures, consensus also would be needed to define '*direct* therapeutic benefit'. Too rigid a distinction between research that offers '*direct* therapeutic benefit' and other research creates a false dichotomy. Sometimes, it is not known initially whether the project will offer *direct* therapeutic benefit. At other times, a project may be undertaken for a purely scientific purpose, and yet may offer the subjects some *indirect* therapeutic benefit. As the Regulations now stand, such *indirect* therapeutic benefit must either be ignored and the research classified solely by its degree of risk, or the research must be classified as offering a *direct* therapeutic benefit which overstates its expected clinical value. The distinction is important as it determines the level of risk that the Regulations permit and whether the child's dissent is binding. The following example illustrates concerns about indirect therapeutic benefits.

In the United States, pharmaceutical tests of new chemotherapeutic compounds are done in four stages. The first phase determines the drug's ability to kill cancer cells in relationship to its potential to kill healthy cells. Even if a drug has been shown to be effective in killing cancer cells in a test tube, questions remain as to whether the compound can kill cancer cells in patients and whether its toxicity will interfere with its potential usefulness. To characterize these trials as offering the prospect of *direct* therapeutic benefit is very misleading. The distinction is critical, because it changes the level of risk that the Regulations permit and whether the child's dissent is binding. If the trials offer the prospect of *direct* therapeutic benefit, parents can authorize their child's participation over the child's dissent, regardless of the level of risk. However, if these trials do not offer any direct therapeutic benefit, children can participate only if the risk entails no more than a minor increase over minimal risk *and* the child assents. I propose the inclusion of another category to accommodate phase I tests which would offer the potential for 'indirect therapeutic benefit',[61] the potential for generalizable knowledge, and would entail no more than a minor increase over minimal risk. I label this category of research §46.406β to emphasize that it is a subset of section 46.406 of the Federal Regulations.

This may be overstating a difference. Research which offers only the potential for indirect benefit may be coercive to families of critically ill children, particularly since there may be no research which does not offer the potential for indirect benefit. The healthy child who participates as a normal control for a research protocol may become critically ill in the future and benefit from the research. To that extent, all research has potential indirect benefit for all subjects. A crucial difference is that the indirect benefits from research in category 46.406β are needed by the subjects immediately.

I propose one further modification to the classification scheme of the Federal Regulations. The Regulations presently classify all minimal risk research under section 46.404. Minimal risk research which offers a direct therapeutic benefit should be classified under section 46.405. The revised classification scheme I propose is depicted in table 5.2.

TABLE 5.2 *Proposed Revisions to the Classification Scheme of the FederalRegulations on Research Involving Children*

Category of Research	Children Unable to Give Assent	Children Capable of Giving Assent
§ 46.404 research, involving minimal risk without the prospect of direct therapeutic benefit		
§ 46.405 research, which offers the prospect of direct therapeutic benefit to the individual subjects. Entails *any degree of risk.*		
§ 46.406 research, which offers no prospect of direct therapeutic benefit* but offers the potential for generalizable knowledge of *vital importance*. Entails no more than a minor increase over minimal risk.		
§ 46.406β research, which offers no prospect of direct therapeutic benefit but offers the potential for generalizable knowledge of *vital importance, and* which offers the prospect of indirect therapeutic benefit. Entails no more than a minor increase over minimal risk.**		
§ 46.407 research, not otherwise approvable, which presents an opportunity to prevent or alleviate serious health problems of children generally. Entails more than a minor increase over minimal risk.		

Note: The original classification scheme appears in 48 Fed. Reg. 9814, at 9818–20 (1983).

* While this research may unexpectedly yield therapeutic benefit, it is neither the intent of the research nor the hope of the subject. In contrast, in category 46.406β research, there is some belief that the research *may* yield immediate therapeutic benefit to the subject.
** Like the category of research defined in section 46.406, category 46.406β research can entail at most a minor increase over minimal risk. Desperate parents may want to authorize their child's participation even when the risks are very high, and are outweighed by the potential benefit. By limiting the amount of risk that this category of research entails, this recommendation seeks to balance the autonomy of the subject (or in the case of children, the autonomy of the subject's parents) with the promotion of the subject's welfare. A research project which entails more than a minor increase over minimal risk, regardless of the prospect of *indirect* benefit, would come under section 46.407.

5. *Informed Consent*

The Federal Regulations require that a research protocol has adequate provisions for the procurement of informed consent. The informed consent standard and process were first described by the courts in *Salgo v. Stanford*.[62] The ruling stated that physicians must disclose to the patient the nature of the illness, the harms, risks, and benefits of the proposed procedure and its alternatives as well as the consequences of refusing treatment. The patient, in turn, must give voluntary consent or refusal. Nine years after *Salgo*, the surgeon general proposed similar guidelines for obtaining informed consent in all research that was federally funded.[63]

Despite these standards, most studies show that patients do not give informed consent for proposed therapies,[64] and subjects give inadequate consent for their participation in research protocols.[65] Many explanations exist why patients and subjects do not give informed consent including the failure of physician-scientists to disclose fully the risks, benefits and alternatives,[66] the tendency of ill persons to conflate the roles of patient and subject and physician and scientist,[67] and the overreliance by physicians on informed consent forms which are unreadable to most patients and subjects.[68]

Failures in the informed consent process lead to serious inequities in research as the process serves as a social filter: better-educated and wealthier individuals are more likely to refuse to participate and are underrepresented in most research.[69] The problem is perpetuated in paediatrics because parents who volunteer their children are less educated and underrepresented in the professional and managerial occupations compared to their non-volunteering counterparts.[70]

The National Commission chose seven years as the age at which children should be included in the consent process. The Commission cited empirical evidence that by seven years, most children have some understanding of the research project and the procedures that they entail. The Commission's guidelines require investigators to explain the procedures to children older than seven years in language which they can understand and then to seek their assent. The Commission held that the child's dissent should be binding unless the research offered direct therapeutic benefit in which case parents could override their child's dissent.[71] Although the Regulations did not adopt strict age limits, it retained the spirit of the Commission's report.[72]

Although the Regulations seek increasing respect for children's decisions as they mature,[73] they do not offer specific guidelines that distinguish between the decisions made by competent and incompetent children. In contrast, I propose a three-tiered classification scheme which can adequately account for children's developing maturity and their evolving role in the consent process. The three categories are (1) the category in which the child is incapable of giving assent (e.g. infants); (2) the category in which the child is capable of giving assent, but is incompetent to give full and effective voluntary consent (e.g. school-aged children); and (3) the category in which the child is capable of giving effective and voluntary consent (e.g. the child in mid- to late adolescence). The value of this three-tiered classification scheme will become clearer when I discuss the distinction between research categorized under section 46.406 and the revision I propose, 46.406β, below.

The proposed classification scheme is shown in table 5.3.

6. *Constrained Parental Autonomy as a Moral Framework that can be Used to Justify Minimal-Risk Research (section 46.404)*

The Regulations permit some research on children which offers no prospect of direct therapeutic benefit to the children subjects. Ramsey argued that a child can never morally participate as a research subject when the research does not offer the prospect of direct therapeutic benefit.[74] His arguments can be refuted using the model of constrained parental autonomy.

Ramsey argues that parents cannot give informed consent for their child's participation in activities which do not directly benefit the child. The argument that parents can consent only to activities which directly benefit their child holds parents to a best interest standard. Two problems with this standard are that it permits too much state intervention and does not allow for parents to balance the needs of the child with the needs of other family members. In reality, parents are not held to a best interest stand-

TABLE 5.3 *Proposed Further Revisions to the Classification Scheme of the Federal Regulations on Research Involving Children*

Category of Research	Children Unable to Give Assent	Children Capable of Giving Assent	Children Capable of Giving Consent
§ 46.404 research, involving minimal risk without the prospect of direct therapeutic benefit			
§ 46.405 research, which offers the prospect of direct therapeutic benefit to the individual subjects. Entails *any degree of risk*.			
§ 46.406 research, which offers no prospect of direct therapeutic benefit but offers the potential for generalizable knowledge of *vital importance*. Entails no more than a minor increase over minimal risk.			
§ 46.406β research, which offers no prospect of direct therapeutic benefit but offers the potential for generalizable knowledge of *vital importance, and* which offers the prospect of indirect therapeutic benefit. Entails no more than a minor increase over minimal risk.			
§ 46.407 research, not otherwise approvable, which presents an opportunity to prevent or alleviate serious health problems of children generally. Entails more than a minor increase over minimal risk.			

Note: The original classification scheme appears in 48 Fed. Reg. 9814, at 9818–20 (1983).

ard because it would be too intrusive into the daily routine of most families. For example, parents often take their children on self-serving errands and excursions and no one suggests that they should not be allowed to do so. Similarly, parents rear their children according to their own religious and cultural beliefs even when they know that the inculcation of minority beliefs and values may reduce or restrict their child's opportunities. In Chapter 3, I argued that parents should have presumptive decision-making authority for their children and that parental autonomy should be questioned only if their decision is disrespectful of the child's developing personhood. This does not mean that the parents' decision is best, only that giving parents wide discretion promotes the child's well-being while respecting both parental autonomy and family autonomy.

Ramsey's second objection that the child's participation does not treat the child as a Kantian person is correct. But children are not full Kantian persons and whether their participation is morally permissible must be based on a modified principle of respect. Parental authorization of their child's participation in research of minimal risk and harm does not necessarily treat the child solely as a means. Rather, parents who value participation in social projects will try to inculcate similar values into their child. It is likely that their child will come to share in some, if not most, of their values. To the extent that the child can be expected to share in such social goals, his participation promotes his life plans even if his assent is unattainable at the time. Even if he never shares in these goals, they are goals which responsible parents may try to inculcate into their child.

To justify a child's participation as a research subject, I must refute Ramsey's arguments and show that the child's participation is consistent with the modified principle of respect. Consider, again, minimal-risk non-therapeutic research. This research presents no more risk than that which a child typically experiences, or using Terrence Ackerman's standard, such research presents no more risk than that which is encountered in many activities to which parents typically expose their children for educational purposes. Many activities in a typical child's life present greater risks, including such routine activities as the participation in contact sports and travelling in the family car. Not only is it impossible to live in a risk-free world, but also it is contrary to the pursuit of a meaningful life plan. The development of autonomy requires that children be allowed to take some risks. Parents are morally and legally authorized to decide which risks their child may take and in what settings. Parental authorization or prohibition of their child's participation in minimal-risk research is not abusive or neglectful, even if the child is forced to participate against his will. Rather, it is one way in which parents can attempt to steer their child's development into a socially responsible adult. They may or may not succeed, but it is reasonable for them to try to guide his development in this way.

This conclusion is at odds with the recommendations of the National Commission and the guidelines of the Federal Regulations.[75] Both recommend that the child's assent or dissent be binding in minimal-risk non-therapeutic research. I am arguing that this recommendation does not pay enough deference to parental autonomy. The model of constrained parental autonomy permits parents to override their child's dissent in minimal risk research if they believe that it will serve to guide his development according to their vision of the good life, realizing that their child may ultimately reject this conception of the good. This may not be the best way for parents to guide their child's development, but the goal is not to define the ideal parent–child relationship. Given a liberal community's tolerance of a wide range of conceptions of the good, state intervention is only justified if the parents' decision is abusive, neglectful, or exploitative, not if an alternative is better.

The arguments presented so far only justify the child's participation in research which entails minimal risk. In the next sections, I consider the impact that the probabilities and degrees of risks and benefits should have on the child's participation and on the child's role in the decision-making process.

7. Whether Utilitarian Arguments can Justify the Child Subject's Participation as a Research Subject

Ramsey sought to prohibit all research that failed to offer direct benefit to the child subject, even if the risks were minimal. I have argued that this position fails to respect parental autonomy. Parents can authorize their child's participation in research which entails minimal risk, even over their child's dissent, without disrespecting the child's personhood. At the other end of the spectrum is section 46.407 of the Federal Regulations, which states that if the risks are more than a minor increase over minimal risk and the research does not offer the prospect of direct benefit (or offers the prospect of benefit that is inadequate to justify the amount of risk), then the research can be justified only if it offers the 'opportunity to understand, prevent, or alleviate a serious problem affecting the health or welfare of children'.[76]

The moral justification for the child's participation in such research is utilitarian; it permits the enrolment of a child as a research subject if the costs (harms and risks) to the child are significantly outweighed by the potential benefit to society at large. This suggests that when the stakes are high enough, the ends may justify the means. Beecher, one of the earliest critics of the morality of human experimentation in the United States wrote: 'An experiment is ethical or not at its inception. It does not become ethical *post hoc*—ends do not justify means.'[77] Like Beecher, I do not believe that a utilitarian argument can justify a child's participation as a research subject. Although the Regulations require strict national review of such research, this protection is inadequate because such research is inconsistent with the modified principle of respect. The U.K. working group on ethics also concluded that the participation of children in this type of research was immoral and emphasized that this was the one substantive disagreement that they had with the Commission's recommendations.[78]

Imagine that a competent child who can give informed consent, consents to participate in such a research project. If a competent child identifies her good with the research goals and willingly sacrifices her own well-being for society at large, then why not permit her participation as we would permit the participation of a competent adult? In Chapter 4, I argued that competent children are not similarly situated with their competent adult counterparts.[79] Empirical data show that consent to serve as a subject of human experimentation is not a random phenomenon. Rather, subjects tend to be less educated, have less-sophisticated medical knowledge, and less frequently hold professional positions compared to those who refuse.[80] Competent children are at a distinct disadvantage in giving an informed refusal in comparison with better-educated adults. As such, competent children can benefit from extra protection, even if they do not want it. Their consent is insufficient. Incompetent children are in need of even greater protection, and so their assent is also inadequate.

Nor can parents authorize their child's participation in this category of research. Although constrained parental autonomy permits parents to balance the risks to one child against the benefits to other family members, the model does not permit such a balance when the risks threaten one child and the benefits are beyond the intimate family. Parents are given wide latitude in balancing the risks and benefits among family members because of the importance of the family's well-being to the parents' and the child(ren)'s well-being. But once parents seek to balance the child's well-being beyond the boundaries of the family, their autonomy ought to be limited. Their focus must be on the individual child's self-regarding interests and developing personhood which are threatened by such research. As such, the potential knowledge to be gained from such research cannot be obtained morally.

Ramsey argued that all non-therapeutic research on children is immoral. He did not prohibit all such research, but concluded that physicians must 'sin bravely'.[81] I argued in section 6 that minimal-risk non-therapeutic research can be performed morally. In contrast, when non-therapeutic research entails more than a minor increase over minimal risk, the participation of children subjects is always immoral and must be prohibited. Review by a national committee is inadequate; the decision to balance the well-being of a particular child against the possibility of large societal benefit is a utilitarian calculus which fails to respect the developing personhood of the child. *All* children should be prohibited from such research, regardless of their competency and despite the utility of the research.

8. *The Intermediate Cases: Sections 46.405, 46.406, and 46.406β*

A. *Section 46.405*

Section 46.405 regulates research which entails more than minimal risk and which offers the prospect of direct therapeutic benefit to the individual subjects. According to the National Commission, parental permission is necessary and sufficient as long as the benefit/risk is as favourable as the alternatives.[82] These cases are the only cases in which the Regulations hold that the child's dissent should not be binding.[83] The recommendations of the Regulations are consistent with the modified principle of respect. Parents are responsible for procuring (and to some extent, defining) their child's basic needs, and health care is one such need. If the parents believe that the child's participation in therapeutic research will promote his basic medical needs, then they must be empowered to authorize it. Their decision to authorize their child's participation in research which offers the prospect of direct therapeutic benefit and which has a benefit/risk as favourable as the non-experimental alternatives is neither neglectful nor abusive. To the extent that the research seeks to determine scientific efficacy, it treats the child as a means, but the research also seeks to promote the child's well-being, which promotes the child's developing personhood, and thus treats the child as an end. Both a Kantian and modified Kantian principle of respect allow individuals to be treated as means if they are simultaneously treated as ends.

If the competent child dissents, the Regulations allow parents to override the competent refusal of their children. When parental autonomy as to what will serve the child's medical well-being is pitted against the competent child's belief of what is in his own interest, the parents' decision trumps because parents have ultimate responsibility for promoting their child's basic medical needs. This does not mean that they should exert their trump card and force their child's participation. Rather, the best outcome would be to achieve family consensus. A good outcome would yield a compromise with which all the parties were satisfied. And yet, when disagreement prevails, there is not necessarily a middle ground. The clinician-investigators must either enrol or not enrol the child in the protocol; they must respect either the parents' consent or the child's refusal.

Constrained parental autonomy operates on the premise that parents have ultimate responsibility for their child's health care even after the child has achieved a threshold of competency. If parents believe that their child should participate in research that offers the prospect of direct therapeutic benefit, then they must have the authority to authorize her participation, even if it means that they override their (competent) child's dissent.

B. *Section 46.406*

Section 46.406 includes research that entails no more than a minor increase over minimal risk and which offers no prospect of direct therapeutic benefit, but which offers the potential for generalizable knowledge of *vital importance*. The Federal Regulations permit parental authorization for children incapable of giving assent. However, if the child is capable of giving assent, then his dissent is binding.

The justification offered by the Regulations for section 46.406 is utilitarian: the potential benefit to children as a class outweighs the costs (harms and risks) to the individual child. It is not adequate to assume that treatment that works in adults will work in children because the metabolism and physiology of children differ in significant ways. Data about children can be obtained only by studying children. I argued in section 7 that it is immoral for children to participate in research which entails more than a minor increase over minimal risk without the prospect of proportionate benefit. Here the research provides no personal benefit, but places the subjects at less risk (no more than a minor increase over minimal risk). Can children morally participate?

In this case, the difference between the child who can give assent and the child who cannot becomes significant. Children who are incapable of giving assent should not be allowed to participate, because their participation uses them for the benefit of society at large while threatening their partially actualized and developing personhood. Their participation is inconsistent with the modified principle of respect. In contrast, if the child who is capable of giving assent (either because he is competent and can give full consent, or because although incompetent, he can give effective assent) gives assent, then his participation respects his partially actualized personhood. While the research uses the child as a means, the child's assent signifies that his participation promotes goals that he identifies as consonant with his ends (without seriously threatening his future well-being). The child's assent makes his participation consistent with the modified principle of respect. Furthermore, by holding his dissent as binding, the child comes to realize that his opinion matters and that he is respected as a partially actualized person, even while his parents are moulding him into the person he will become.

But the child's assent alone is not and should not be sufficient. Parental permission is necessary to ensure the relative safety of the research, to protect the child from possible abuse, and to protect the child from his own inexperience. In addition, parents should retain the right to prohibit such participation because they have ultimate responsibility for the physical, psychological, and financial harms that the participation may cause. Both the parents and the child must agree to the child's participation.

To allow children who can give effective assent to participate in such research does not undermine the potential risks and harms. They are typical of the degree of risks which children confront frequently. Many activities that involve risks have valuable purposes (whether it be personal physical fitness or the chance to advance scientific knowledge). Children should be encouraged but not compelled to participate in this type of research, lest the distinction between obligatory and supererogatory is lost. The dissent of the child or the parent makes the child's participation immoral despite its utilitarian value.

This does not mean that an IRB must always permit all children capable of giving assent the opportunity to participate in a research project classified under section 46.406. The Federal Regulations recommend that research be performed first on animal models, then on adults, and on older children before younger children. The rationale was that adults and older children are more capable of understanding the risks and benefits, and their consent is more expressive of their true needs, wants, and interests. In light of these recommendations, an IRB can suggest that a research protocol be modified so that the subjects will be drawn from an older paediatric population (i.e. from those who can give consent and not merely assent). Similarly, an IRB can classify the risks of a protocol differently for different populations of children. For example, the IRB can characterize the risks to younger children as 'more than a minor increase over minimal risk' but characterize the risks to older children as only a 'minor increase over minimal risk'. Then, the research would fall under section 46.406 for older children and section 46.407 for younger children which would require different standards of scrutiny.[84]

C. *Proposed Section 46.406β*

The enrolment of a terminally ill child into a phase I chemotherapeutic trial is research that falls under what I term category 46.406β. Phase I research is performed to determine drug toxicity and offers, albeit indirectly, the prospect of therapeutic benefit which are rare and often small. Specifically, subjects who receive phase I drugs rarely achieve complete remission, but may increase their survival by a short interval.[85] In deciding whether to authorize a child's participation, parents must determine whether the benefit/risk is sufficient and whether the risks and harms are justifiable. Given the experimental nature of the trial, the parents' decision either to authorize or to refuse to authorize their child's participation is moral. Parents may come to opposite conclusions for a variety of reasons. One parent may believe that her child has suffered enough and may not want to subject him to more medical interventions, although it is the child's only chance, albeit a remote one, of surviving. Another parent may enrol her child because she believes that, within reason, everything should be done to promote her child's well-being, while her spouse may consent to the child's enrolment to give meaning to what he perceives to be pointless suffering.

While the prospect of *direct* therapeutic benefit permits parents to authorize the participation of their children, including those unable to assent to participate, does the prospect of *indirect* therapeutic benefit give them such wide leeway? If so, there is an important difference between research that falls under section 46.406 and 46.406β regulations, as infants would be prohibited from participating in the former but would be permitted to participate in the latter. To this extent, the new classification is dangerous because it encourages vague claims of potential indirect therapeutic benefit to justify the enrolment of young children. But this does not make the distinction immoral. Rather, it only confirms the importance of IRB review to ensure that research which does not offer *indirect* therapeutic benefit to the particular subject is classified as category 46.406, not 46.406β.

I have argued that the potential for therapeutic benefit increases parental authority and diminishes the role of the child's dissent. Given the difficulty that most competent adults have in understanding the uncertainty and risks of research protocols, it is unrealistic to assume that an incompetent child's dissent expresses adequate understanding of indirect benefit. Participation in research which has the potential for indirect therapeutic benefit may be the child's only chance for survival. It can have significant therapeutic value, even if its likelihood is remote. Parents who override their incompetent child's dissent in these situations act in accordance with the modified principle of respect. They ignore their child's present autonomy in order to promote his basic health needs. The parents may be misguided in their deliberations about the therapeutic value of the protocol, but constrained parental autonomy maintains that where reasonable persons can disagree, parental autonomy should be respected.

But when the child is competent, parents should not be allowed to override their child's competent dissent in research which offers only the prospect of *indirect* therapeutic benefit. As risks increase and benefits decrease, the balance does not always favour strict parental autonomy. Rather, the modified principle of respect requires that the competent child's dissent is binding in research that falls under category 46.406β.

Imagine, then, a child whose cancer has failed to respond to standard treatment and who is a candidate for a phase I trial. The oncologist-investigator explains that the purpose of the test is to determine toxicity, and will require many blood tests that will not benefit the child directly. On the up side, he explains that over 5 per cent of children have medically benefited from similar participation.[86] The parents give their permission; the child dissents. The child understands that he is dying, but maintains that he has suffered enough and does not want to be a pincushion. This child, unlike the incompetent child, can understand that the likelihood that this treatment will promote his basic health needs is remote and that the true benefit, if it exists, is to future generations. Similarly, he can understand the costs of participation better than most of us, based on his experience with side-effects of other cancer regimens. Given that the research is not expected to benefit him directly, his participation over his dissent would override his partially actualized personhood without realistic expectations of promoting his future personhood (the child is dying). Respect prohibits his participation. In research of this class, the consent of both the parent and the competent child are necessary and the dissent of either ought to be binding.

9. *Conclusion*

In this chapter, I have addressed three important issues regarding the participation of children as research subjects. First, contra

TABLE 5.4 *Proposed Further Revisions to the Classification Scheme of the Federal Regulations on Research Involving Children*

Category of Research	Children Unable to Give Assent	Children Capable of Giving Assent	Children Capable of Giving Consent
§ 46.404 research, involving minimal risk without the prospect of direct therapeutic benefit	Parental permission is necessary and sufficient.	Parental permission is necessary and sufficient.	Parental permission is necessary and sufficient.
§ 46.405 research, which offers the prospect of direct therapeutic benefit to the individual subjects. Entails *any degree of risk.*	Parental permission is necessary and sufficient.	Parental permission is necessary and sufficient.	Parental permission is necessary and sufficient.
§ 46.406 research, which offers no prospect of direct therapeutic benefit but offers the potential for generalizable knowledge of *vital importance.* Entails no more than a minor increase over minimal risk.	Research is impermissible.	Parental permission and the child's assent are required.	Parental permission and the child's assent are required.
§ 46.406β research, which offers no prospect of direct therapeutic benefit but offers the potential for generalizable knowledge of *vital importance, and* which offers the prospect of indirect therapeutic benefit. Entails no more than a minor increase over minimal risk.	Parental permission is necessary and sufficient.	Parental permission is necessary and sufficient.	Parental permission and the child's assent are required.
§ 46.407 research, not otherwise approvable, which presents an opportunity to prevent or alleviate serious health problems of children generally. Entails more than a minor increase over minimal risk.	Research is impermissible.	Research is impermissible.	Research is impermissible.

Note: The original classification scheme appears in 48 Fed. Reg. 9814, at 9818–20 (1983).

Ramsey, I have argued that children can morally participate in some research which offers no direct therapeutic benefit. Second, there may be some knowledge that would be valuable to future generations that cannot be learned without exploiting children. National review is not sufficient protection, and such research should be prohibited until methods are developed that will not exploit children subjects. Third, although respect for children requires that they are included in the decision-making process, respect for parental autonomy requires that the child's dissent is binding in fewer cases than the Federal Regulations authorize.

The questions of when children can morally participate as subjects of human experimentation and whether their dissent should be binding help demonstrate how a modified principle of respect can serve as a guiding principle for decision making for children in the research setting. In table 5.4 I offer final revisions to the Federal Regulations' guidelines regarding the participation of children in human experimentation that are consistent with my model of constrained parental autonomy.

Notes

1. Nuremberg Code, 1946, Principle 1, reprinted in W. T. Reich (ed.), *Encyclopedia of Bioethics*, iv (New York: Free Press, 1978), 1764.
2. See, for example, 18th World Medical Association, 'Declaration of Helsinki: Recommendations Guiding Medical Doctors in Biomedical Research Involving Human Subjects', Helsinki, Finland, 1964 (revised most recently by the 41st World Medical Association in Hong Kong, September 1989). Both the British Medical Association (BMA) and the American Medical Association (AMA) have published ethical guidelines as well. 'Experimental Research on Human Beings' was drafted by the BMA in 1963 and 'Ethical Guidelines for Clinical Investigation' was published by the AMA in 1966. Both have since been revised and expanded to address other ethical concerns of medical practice.
3. The phrase 'non-therapeutic research' implies that the research has a purely scientific purpose and offers no therapeutic (clinical) function in contrast with 'therapeutic research', which implies that the research has both scientific and clinical goals. In practice, the distinction is not clear-cut. Although there are research projects which offer no therapeutic benefits to the subjects (e.g. when a healthy volunteer is paid to participate in a study to determine the metabolism and

excretion rate of a new compound), many research projects offer therapeutic benefits, even if only indirectly. In addition, activities commonly referred to as 'therapeutic research' often entail procedures which do not directly benefit the subject (e.g. the process of randomization in clinical trials). The National Commission for the Protection of Human Subjects of Biomedical and Behavioral Research sought to be more precise by using the notion of research which does or does not offer the prospect of direct benefit. The U.K. Institute of Medical Ethics working group on the ethics of clinical research investigations on children found the National Commission's phrases unwieldy and chose to use the terms 'therapeutic' and 'non-therapeutic' for their simplicity and utility. R. H. Nicholson (ed.), *Medical Research with Children: Ethics, Law, and Practice* (Oxford: Oxford University Press, 1986), 26–31. I use the National Commission's phrasing except in response to Ramsey.

4. P. Ramsey, *The Patient as Person* (New Haven, Conn.: Yale University Press, 1970), esp. 11–19.

5. R. A. McCormick, 'Proxy Consent in the Experimentation Situation', *Perspectives in Biology and Medicine*, 18 (1974), 11.

6. McCormick, 'Proxy Consent', 9.

7. McCormick, 'Proxy Consent', 11–12.

8. McCormick, 'Proxy Consent', 12. Of note, McCormick was willing to impose a minimal positive sociability upon competent adults as well (McCormick, 'Proxy Consent', 12–13).

9. P. Ramsey, 'Children as Research Subject: A Reply', *Hastings Center Report*, 7 (1977), 40.

10. P. Ramsey, 'The Enforcement of Morals: Non-Therapeutic Research on Children', *Hastings Center Report*, 6 (1976), 24.

11. I. Kant, *Grounding for the Metaphysics of Morals* (1785) trans. J. W. Ellington (Indianapolis, Ind.: Hackett Publishing, 1981), paragraph 429.

12. R. A. McCormick, 'Experimentation in Children: Sharing in Sociality', *Hastings Center Report*, 6 (1976), 43.

13. McCormick, 'Experimentation', 42.

14. The phrase was coined by H. Shirkey in 1963, according to J. D. Lockhart, 'Pediatric Drug Testing: Is it at Risk?' *Hastings Center Report*, 7 (1977), 8. It refers to those persons with rare conditions that do not receive adequate clinical study and understanding. The result is that clinicians treat these subject-patients using unproven therapies. So, for example, if new medicines could not be tested on children, then paediatricians would have to rely on adult data which may or may not be appropriate for children, who metabolize drugs differently.

15. Ramsey, 'The Enforcement of Morals', 21, citing 'Medical Progress

and Canons of Loyalty to Experimental Subjects', *Proceedings of Conference on Biological Revolution/Theological Impact*, sponsored by the Institute for Theological Encounter with Science and Technology, Fordyce House, St Louis, Missouri (6–8 April 1973), 51–77.

16. H. K. Beecher, *Research and the Individual* (Boston: Little, Brown, 1970), 63.

17. W. G. Bartholome, 'Parents, Children, and the Moral Benefits of Research', *Hastings Center Report*, 6 (1976), 44–5.

18. T. F. Ackerman, 'Fooling Ourselves with Child Autonomy and Assent in Nontherapeutic Clinical Research', *Clinical Research*, 27 (1979), 345.

19. W. J. Curran and H. K. Beecher, 'Experimentation in Children: A Reexamination of Legal Ethical Principles', *Journal of the American Medical Association*, 210 (1969), 77–83.

20. Bartholome, 'Moral Benefits', 44–5. The term 'assent' can be used to refer to both the incompetent and competent child's agreement to participate in his health care plans. In contrast, the term 'consent' refers *only* to an agreement given by a competent person. Consent meets legal standards whereas assent does not. However, by saying that a (competent) child gave his consent, I do not mean to imply that the competent child's consent or refusal needs to be legally binding, only that it meets legal standards.

21. Ackerman, 'Fooling Ourselves', 346–7. Two empirical studies which validate his arguments are A. H. Schwartz, 'Children's Concepts of Research Hospitalization', *New England Journal of Medicine*, 287 (1972), 589–92; and R. Abramovitch, J. L. Freedman, K. Thoden, and C. Nikolich, 'Children's Capacity to Consent to Participation in Psychological Research: Empirical Findings', *Child Development*, 62 (1991), 1100–9.

22. Ackerman, 'Fooling Ourselves', 345.

23. However, Ackerman challenges his own position later in the article when he writes, '[W]e should respect an intractable objection by the child particularly if it is based upon anxiety or fear which cannot be allayed regarding an experimental procedure.' 'Fooling Ourselves', 348.

24. German Reich, 'Circular of the Ministry of the Interior on Directives Concerning New Medical Treatments and Scientific Experiments on Man', (1931) translated in *International Digest of Health Legislation* (Geneva), 31 (1980), 408–11.

25. National Commission for the Protection of Human Subjects, *Report and Recommendations: Research Involving Children* (Washington, DC: U.S. Government Printing Office, 1977), 2–3.

26. Department of Health, Education, and Welfare (45 C.F.R., part 46), 'Protection of Human Subjects: Proposed Regulations on Research

Involving Children', *Federal Register*, 43 (July 21, 1978), 31,786–94. Cites to the *Federal Register* will hereinafter be abbreviated in the form 43 Fed. Reg. 31,786–94 (1978).

27. Department of Health and Human Services (45 C.F.R., part 46), 'Additional Protections for Children Involved as Subjects in Research', 48 Fed. Reg. 9814–20 (1983). The guidelines for human experimentation were revised again in 1991, although the only change with respect to children concerned exemptions which I do not discuss in this book. See 56 Fed. Reg. 28,032 (1991).

28. Medical Research Council, 'Responsibility in Investigations on Human Subjects', *Report of the Medical Research Council for the year 1962–3* (London: Her Majesty's Stationery Office, 1964), 21–5; Royal College of Physicians, *Supervision of the Ethics of Clinical Research Investigations in Institutions* (London: Royal College of Physicians, 1973); Department of Health and Social Security (DHSS), *Supervision of the Ethics of Clinical Research Investigations and Fetal Research*, HSC(IS) 153 (London: DHHS, 1975); British Paediatric Association (BPA), 'Guidelines to Aid Ethical Committees Considering Research Involving Children', *Archives of Diseases of Childhood*, 55 (1980), 75–7.

29. Nicholson, *Medical Research with Children*.

30. Medical Research Council, Working Party on Research on Children, *The Ethical Conduct of Research on Children* (London: Medical Research Council, 1991); British Paediatric Association, *Guidelines for the Ethical Conduct of Medical Research Involving Children* (London: BPA, 1992).

31. National Commission, *Research Involving Children*, 1–2. The report of the working group on ethics offers a similar argument: '[R]esearch on children is desirable and necessary in order to promote the health and well-being of children.' Nicholson, *Medical Research with Children*, 231.

32. National Commission, *Research Involving Children*, 2.

33. National Commission, *Research Involving Children*, 2–3. See also 46 Fed. Reg. 404 (1983).

34. Institutional review boards (IRBs) serve the primary purpose of protecting the rights and welfare of human research subjects. The first federal document to propose committee review of research procedures was dated 17 November 1953 and 'applied only to intramural research at the newly opened clinical center at the NIH [National Institutes of Health]'. Subcommittee on Health of the Committee on Labor and Public Welfare, U.S. Senate, 'Federal Regulation of Human Experimentation', No. 45-273-0 (Washington DC: U.S. Government Printing Office, 1975), as cited by R. J. Levine, *Ethics and Regulation of Clinical Research*, 2nd ed. (New Haven, Conn.: Yale University Press, 1986), 322. The first federal policy was not issued for another decade. On 8 February 1966, the surgeon general issued a memorandum

requiring prior review of all research involving human subjects funded by U.S. Public Health Service Grants. W. H. Steward, 'Clinical Investigations Using Human Subjects', memorandum dated 8 February 1966, cited by Levine, *Ethics and Regulation*, 323.

Initially most IRB committees were composed of scientists and physicians. Revisions in U.S. Public Health Service policy and DHEW and DHHS regulations have evolved to *require* a more diverse composition. The duties of the IRBs have also expanded. The history of IRBs is given in Levine, *Ethics and Regulation*, Chap. 14.

35. The British Paediatric Association used the terms 'negligible', 'minimal', and 'more than minimal' [risk] in its 1980 document (British Paediatric Association, 'Guidelines to Aid Ethical Committees Considering Research Involving Children'). In 1992, it changed the terms to read 'minimal', 'low', and 'high' (British Paediatric Association, *Guidelines* [1992], 9). despite the recommendations of the working group on ethics to use the terminology used by the U.S. National Commission (Nicholson, *Medical Research with Children*, 105 ff.).

36. National Commission, *Research Involving Children*, p. xx.

37. 46 Fed. Reg. 404 (1983).

38. As the regulations are written, research which entails minimal risk and offers a direct therapeutic benefit is classified as minimal risk research (46 Fed. Reg. 404). I argue in section 5 that by the National Commission's own standards, such research should be classified under research that presents the prospect of direct therapeutic benefit (46 Fed. Reg. 405).

39. 46 Fed. Reg. 405.

40. 46 Fed. Reg. 406.

41. 46 Fed. Reg. 406.

42. 46 Fed. Reg. 407a.

43. 46 Fed. Reg. 407b.

44. National Commission, *Research Involving Children*, 13. The working group on ethics recommends the same age. (Nicholson, *Medical Research with Children*, 149–51.)

45. National Commission, *Research Involving Children*, 16.

46. 46 Fed. Reg. 408.

47. 46 Fed. Reg. 408c. The classic example is if the condition falls under the specialized consent statutes. I argue in Chapter 8 that the specialized consent statutes inappropriately exclude parental involvement. Likewise, I reject the exclusion of parental consent for research done on these conditions.

48. 46 Fed. Reg. 408c.

49. National Commission, *Research Involving Children*, p. xx.

50. R. Thompson, 'Vulnerability in Research: A Developmental Perspective on Research Risk', *Child Development*, 61 (1990), 7.

51. Thompson, 'Vulnerability', 7.

52. Intrathecal medication is drug delivered directly into the cerebrospinal fluid (the fluid around the brain and spinal cord). This is achieved by performing a spinal tap (lumbar puncture) and injecting the medicine through the needle. This creates a high concentration of the drug in the cerebrospinal fluid, which is the intended target.

53. This does not mean that the child who has been treated for cancer can never participate as a research subject. In fact, his cancer treatment was most likely part of an experimental protocol. In addition, his parents may want to encourage his participation if the research is being done to advance knowledge which may be to the child's own benefit, albeit indirectly. My point is only to remind us of this child's increased vulnerability due to his previous illness. He and his family may feel compelled to help the physician in his own research out of a sense of debt.

54. T. F. Ackerman, 'Moral Duties of Investigators Toward Sick Children', *IRB: A Review of Human Subjects Research*, 3 (June/July 1981), 4.

55. T. F. Ackerman, 'Moral Duties of Parents and Non-Therapeutic Research Procedures Involving Children', *Bioethics Quarterly*, 2 (1980), 94–111, as cited in S. L. Leikin, 'An Ethical Issue in Biomedical Research: The Involvement of Minors in Informed and Third Party Consent', *Clinical Research*, 31 (1983), 38.

56. National Commission, *Research Involving Children*, 8–9.

57. J. Janofsky and B. Starfield, 'Assessment of Risk in Research on Children', *Journal of Pediatrics*, 98 (1981), 842–6.

58. A. Lascari, 'Risks of Research in Children', *Journal of Pediatrics*, 98 (1981), 759–60.

59. P. Williams, 'Success in Spite of Failure: Why IRBs Falter in Reviewing Risks and Benefits', *IRB: A Review of Human Subjects Research*, 6 (May/June 1984), 1–4.

60. Williams, 'Why IRBs Falter', 3, citing J. A. F. Stoner, 'A Comparison of Individual and Group Decisions Involving Risk', M.S. thesis, School of Industrial Management, Massachusetts Institute of Technology, 1961.

61. By '*indirect* therapeutic benefit' I mean that the intent of the research is not to offer therapeutic benefit, although the conditions of the research make such a benefit possible.

62. Salgo v. Leland Stanford Jr., University Board of Trustees, 317 P.2d 170 (Cal. Dist. Ct. App., 1957).

63. Surgeon general, memorandum, 'Clinical Investigations.'

64. W. A. Silverman, 'The Myth of Informed Consent in Daily Practice and

in Clinical Trials', *Journal of Medical Ethics*, 15 (1989), 6–11; and J. Katz, *The Silent World of Doctor and Patient* (New York: Free Press, 1984).

65. See Silverman, 'The Myth', and A. L. Schultz, G. P. Pardee, and J. W. Ensinck, 'Are Research Subjects Really Informed?' *Western Journal of Medicine*, 123 (1975), 76–80.

66. J. Katz, 'Why Doctors Don't Disclose Uncertainty', *Hastings Center Report*, 14 (February 1984), 35–44.

67. Katz, *The Silent World*.

68. See, for example, M. T. Baker and H. A. Taub, 'Readability of Informed Consent Forms for Research in a Veterans Administration Medical Center', *JAMA*, 250 (1983), 2646–8; T. M. Grunder, 'On the Readability of Surgical Consent Forms', *New England Journal of Medicine*, 302 (1980), 900–2; and K. J. Tarnowski, D. M. Allen, C. Mayhall, and P. A. Kelly, 'Readability of Pediatric Biomedical Research Informed Consent Forms', *Pediatrics*, 85 (1990), 58–62.

69. Silverman, 'The Myth'.

70. S. C. Harth, R. R. Johnstone, and Y. H. Thong, 'The Psychological Profile of Parents Who Volunteer Their Children for Clinical Research: A Controlled Study', *Journal of Medical Ethics*, 18 (1992), 86–93.

71. This is why I believe that minimal risk research which offers the potential for direct therapeutic benefit should be classified under 46 Fed. Reg. 405 (1983). The Commission recommended that parents *always* be allowed to override their child's dissent when the research has therapeutic potential (i.e. when research falls under section 46.405). In contrast, the Commission held that the child's dissent in minimal risk research should be binding (i.e. when research falls under section 46.404). Because parents can override their child's dissent in research which entails minimal risk but which also has the prospect of direct therapeutic benefit, it would be better to classify it under section 46.405.

72. The working group on ethics also recommended seven years of age (Nicholson, *Medical Research with Children*, 235), although the new BPA and Medical Research Council (MRC) guidelines do not offer a specific age.

73. National Commission, *Research Involving Children*, 16.

74. In the terms of the classification scheme proposed in table 5.3, Ramsey's claim is that children should participate in research only if it offers the potential for direct benefit (46 Fed. Reg. 405), and that their participation in all other research is immoral. Specifically, Ramsey denies that children can morally participate in minimal-risk research that does not offer the prospect of direct therapeutic benefit (46 Fed. Reg. 404).

75. It is also against the conclusions of the working group on ethics, the BPA, and the MRC.

76. 46 Fed. Reg. 407.

77. H. K. Beecher, 'Ethics and Clinical Research', *New England Journal of Medicine*, 274 (1966), 1360.

78. Nicholson, *Medical Research with Children*, 14.

79. Other ethicists who write that competent children are not similarly situated with their adult counterparts are L. M. Purdy, *In Their Best Interest? The Case Against Equal Rights for Children* (New York: Cornell University Press, 1992), 76–84, and W. Gaylin, 'Competence: No Longer All or None', in W. Gaylin and R. Macklin (eds.), *Who Speaks for the Child: The Problems of Proxy Consent* (New York: Plenum Press, 1982), 27–54.

80. Silverman, 'The Myth'.

81. P. Ramsey, 'The Enforcement of Morals: Nontherapeutic Research on Children', *Hastings Center Report*, 6 (1976), 21.

82. Although the working group on ethics came to the same conclusion, they also permit the competent child to give consent for his participation without the need for parental permission. (Nicholson, *Medical Research with Children*, 151.)

83. This is not quite accurate. Although this category is the only category in which the child's dissent is not binding, a local IRB can decide that a particular research protocol does not require the child's assent, or that the child's dissent is not binding. See 46 Fed. Reg. 408. The working group on ethics came to the same conclusion for all children below the age of fourteen. When children are fourteen years or older, they held that the 'adolescent subject's refusal to give consent, whether to therapeutic or non-therapeutic research procedures, should be binding'. (Nicholson, *Medical Research with Children*, 151.) The MRC guidelines state that the Family Law Reform Act 1969 gives sixteen-year-olds full power to consent to medical treatment and that therapeutic research is a form of medical treatment, so children sixteen years and older can consent to participate in research without parental permission. Nevertheless, if there is some doubt as to the competency of the child, parental permission can be sought and parental objection should be given 'considerable weight'. Medical Research Council, *The Ethical Conduct*, section 7.2.4.

84. Actually, I argued in section 7 above that research which falls under section 46.407 is always impermissible so the different classifications for different ages effectively means that only older children would be allowed to participate.

85. A compilation of 1,248 subjects in phase I trials sponsored by the National Cancer Institute between 1974 and 1982 yielded an overall

complete plus partial response rate of 2.9 per cent. See E. Estey et al., 'Therapeutic Response in Phase I Trials of Antineoplastic Agents', *Cancer Treatment Reports*, 70 (1986), 1105–15. Of note, only two patients (0.16 per cent) achieved total remission.

The data are slightly more promising in children. A cumulative review of all children enrolled into phase I studies of chemotherapeutic agents conducted by investigators at St Jude Children's Research Hospital and within the Pediatric Oncology Group Institutions between 1967 and 1989 found a 5.9 per cent chance of therapeutic benefit for a child who participates in a phase I clinical trial. See W. L. Furman et al., 'Mortality in Pediatric Phase I Clinical Trials', *Journal of the National Cancer Institute*, 81 (1989), 1193–4. The researchers did not distinguish between response and remission. Even if one assumes that paediatric patients do better than adults, complete remission would still be very rare.

86. See Furman et al., 'Phase I Clinical Trials'.

6

The Child as Organ Donor

1. A Brief Legal History of Paediatric Organ Donations

The first successful kidney transplants from living donors occurred in 1957 when three minors served as kidney donors for their identical twin siblings.[1] Seeking to insulate the hospital from liability, attorneys requested the Massachusetts Supreme Judicial Court to review the planned procedures.[2] The attorneys' concerns were twofold: the common law principles prohibited minor donors from giving effective consent to medical procedures; and it was not clear whether parents could give consent for their child to participate as an organ donor because the donation was not undertaken to serve the child's medical well-being. The Supreme Judicial Court sought neither to lower the age of authority nor to redefine parental power. Rather, it developed a special procedure by which courts could authorize such transplants.[3] Although the court did not articulate a consistent standard for ascertaining the conditions upon which such authorization would be appropriate, the justices pointed to the extraordinary benefit to the recipient, the minimal risk to the donor,[4] the parents' consent, the donor's consent, and the existence of some benefit to the donor. In fact, in each of these cases, the court concluded that the donation was in the donor's best interest.[5] The court acknowledged that the donor did not physically benefit from the donation, but it accepted psychological testimony that claimed that the procedure offered great psychological benefits to the donor, or at least would prevent the serious emotional trauma that would develop if he were not permitted to donate. For example, in *Masden v. Harrison*, Judge Counihan cited the psychological testimony as adequate proof that the operation would serve the donor's best interest:

I am satisfied from the testimony of the psychiatrist that grave emotional impact may be visited upon Leonard [the prospective donor] if the defendants refuse to perform this operation and Leon [the prospective recipient] should die, as apparently he will. See Brown v. Board of Education 347 U.S. 483, 493–494. Such emotional disturbance could well affect the health and physical well-being of Leonard [the prospective donor] for the remainder of his life. I therefore find that this operation is necessary for the continued good health and future well-being of Leonard [the prospective donor] and that in performing the operation the defendants are conferring a benefit upon Leonard [the prospective donor] as well as upon Leon [the prospective recipient].[6]

Following these decisions, the Supreme Judicial Court of Massachusetts granted permission for another two dozen donations over the next twenty years. Many other courts have also allowed parents to authorize the donation of a kidney from an incompetent child for his sibling. Many of these cases have been justified under a best interest standard.[7] In one case, however, the court rejected the goal of determining the donor's best interest, stating that the best interest claim was too speculative.[8] Instead, in *Nathan v. Farinelli*, the court stated that its role was not to determine what was in the potential child donor's best interest, but only to determine whether the parents took all the risks and benefits into consideration. Because the parents did, the court argued that the parents' decision should be binding.

I agree with the *Farinelli* decision not to hold parents to a best interest standard; I disagree that it is sufficient to determine that parents have considered all the risks and benefits because there may be cases in which the risks are too great even if they can be outweighed by the potential benefits. Instead, the parents should make decisions that are consistent with the modified principle of respect. I will use the model of constrained parental autonomy to determine when it is morally justifiable for children to serve as organ donors, and to determine whose consent is necessary.[9]

2. *The Child Donor and Intrafamilial Donations*

Organ donations by living donors can be classified into two categories, based on the likelihood and degree of risk and harm: donations which entail minimal to a minor increase over minimal risk, and donations which entail more than a minor increase over minimal risk. The classification is somewhat arbitrary, as the risks and harms associated with organ donations span a continuum, depending on the organ to be donated. The classification depends on such factors as the procedural risks that the harvest entails (e.g. the type of anaesthesia), the reversibility of the donation (e.g. bone marrow replenishes in several months, whereas a kidney is never regenerated), and the long-term morbidity.

For example, the donation of a pint of blood is a donation of minimal risk. At most, the donation entails the risk of a small bruise and slight fatigue. The risk of long-term sequelae is negligible as blood replenishes itself in several weeks. In comparison, a bone marrow donation is a donation that entails a minor increase over minimal risk. The greatest risk of bone marrow donation lies in the need to undergo general anaesthesia.[10] The aspiration can require over a hundred attempts with a long needle into different bones in the body. During the harvest, there is a small risk that nerves will be injured, possibly permanently. The donor is also at a slightly increased risk of infection for several months until the bone marrow replenishes.

Kidney donations are donations of more than a minor increase over minimal risk. They require general anaesthesia. The harvest requires major abdominal surgery, and both major and minor perioperative complications occur, even when performed by experienced physicians.[11] The recuperation period lasts about six weeks, longer if there are perioperative complications. Late major complications have also been reported.[12]

To determine whether a child's participation respects a child's developing and partially actualized personhood, I need to distinguish between the child donor who is competent and the child donor who is incompetent to consent to participate.[13] A child is competent to make decisions regarding his participation as an organ donor if he understands the risks and benefits of donating, and can decide voluntarily whether to participate.

The classification of children as potential donors is depicted in table 6.1. I will now consider whether such donations are permissible between siblings and whose consent is necessary.

Case I

Suppose, for example, that Paul White, a two-year-old child with leukaemia, needs a bone marrow transplant, and his six-year-old

TABLE 6.1 *Classification of Children as Organ Donors*

Type of Donation	Incompetent Children	Competent Children
Organ donations that entail minimal to minor increase over minimal risks and harms (e.g. blood donation and bone marrow donations, respectively)	Case I	Case IV
Organ donations that entail more than a minor increase over minimal risks and harms (e.g. kidney donations)	Case II	Case III

sister Ann is the best donor candidate. According to the model of constrained parental autonomy, the Whites can authorize Ann to serve as a bone marrow donor if their authorization is consistent with the modified principle of respect. The modified principle of respect permits parents to use their child as a means as long as they *simultaneously* respect the child as the developing person that she is. In intimate families, the well-being of one child is intertwined with the well-being of other family members. Ann is being used as a means to promote her brother's well-being, but this serves to promote the well-being of the family (on which her own well-being depends). As such, her participation serves her own goals, albeit indirectly.[14] The modified principle of respect permits parents to place their child at some medical risk in order to promote other goals provided that the parents do not sacrifice *any* of the child's *basic* needs. Given the low risk of long-term sequelae, the Whites' decision satisfies this condition.

Should Ann be asked whether she assents to the donation? As the case has been defined, we can assume that she is not competent to understand the risks and benefits that the donation entails. Although Ann's parents and the transplant doctors should try to explain to Ann, in language that she can understand, what they are planning to do, her assent is not necessary and her dissent is not binding. Optimally they would procure her assent. Her dissent should alert her parents and physicians to the need for further explanation. Nevertheless, her persistent dissent can be overridden because her parents can promote family goals that conflict with the goals of individual members, provided that they do not sacrifice any of Ann's basic needs.

Case II

Consider Steve Black, a twelve-year-old with chronic renal failure who is doing poorly on dialysis. The physician explains to the family that Steve needs a kidney transplant. Neither parent is a potential candidate because of poor health. The only close relative is a six-year-old sibling, Jim, who is incapable of understanding the risks and harms that a kidney donation entails. Is parental authorization of a kidney donation by an incompetent child for his sibling respectful of the child's developing personhood?

I do not believe it is. Parents should be allowed to authorize a child's participation in intrafamilial donations that entail minimal to a minor increase over minimal risk. Such transplants promote the well-being of the child recipient which, in turn, promotes the well-being of the family, on which the child donor's well-being depends. However, donations that entail significant risks and harms, seriously threaten the developing person that the child is becoming. Although I have argued in favour of parents in deciding what is best for the family as a whole, I have also argued that parents cannot sacrifice one child for the family as a whole: parents must promote the family's well-being as well as the well-being of *each* individual child member. Parents can compromise their child's ideal health interests for a sibling, but they cannot sacrifice one child for another. Since serving as a kidney donor puts the donor child at significant risk for long-term morbidity and mortality, it is disrespectful, even if well intentioned. The Blacks cannot morally authorize Jim to serve as a kidney donor for Steve.

Case III

But does this mean that a child should never be allowed to participate as a kidney donor? Although one might claim that we should exclude all children from serving as kidney donors in order to minimize non-therapeutic health risks, such a blanket prohibition fails to appreciate how family intimacy can be crucial to the enjoyment and further development of the child's own vision of the good life.

Consider the competent child who is capable of understanding the risks and benefits involved in a donation which entails significant risks and harms. What if she voluntarily consents to participate, free from parental coercion?[15] She is competent, and can understand the seriousness of the risks if fully disclosed. Her voluntary participation does not negate the risks, but competent individuals can decide to take even significant risks to achieve important goals. If the existence and promotion of the intimate family and its goals are an important component of an individual's identity and vision of the good life, then the opportunity to serve as an organ donor will be valued. What appears to be significant sacrifice from an impersonal (third-party) perspective is perceived by the potential donor as serving needs integral to her goals. From the donor's intimate perspective, the donation serves personal goals defined to include both her sibling and her sibling's goals. If the competent child judges that the donation does not treat her *solely* as a means but also promotes her well-being, her participation is consistent with the modified principle of respect.

The competent child, however, *is not and should not be authorized* to independently consent to participate as an organ donor which exposes her to significant risk or harm. Parents are still ultimately responsible for their child and must have the right to prohibit such participation. Both the parents and the child must consent to the child's participation in an activity that is disrespectful unless voluntarily undertaken. A dissent by either party ought to be binding.

Contrast the competent child's participation as a kidney donor with her participation in research. In Chapter 5, I argued that the competent child's participation in research that entails more than a minor increase over minimal risk and that does not offer the prospect of direct therapeutic benefit was impermissible because the child's participation was exploitative even if she and her parents gave their consent.[16] In contrast, the competent child's participation as an organ donor is permissible even if the donation threatens her developing personhood. The difference does not depend upon the child's competency, but rather, on the balance between risks and benefits to the child and the family versus the risks and benefits to the child and the larger community. While the child's participation has the potential to be exploitative, risks that would be unacceptable outside of the intimate family context can be permissible if voluntarily undertaken within the family.

Case IV

Suppose, now, that Paul White, the two-year-old-child with leukaemia, has another sibling, a fourteen-year-old brother named John who is a good donor candidate. Can the Whites authorize John's participation as a bone marrow donor? I argued in case I that the Whites can authorize their incompetent daughter's participation in such donations, even if she dissents. If John has achieved a threshold level of competency, is his consent necessary?

The modified principle of respect would encourage John's parents and the physicians to explain to John why his participation is necessary and to explore his questions and concerns. Usually children accept their parents' suggestion, in part, out of concern for their sibling, and in part, in deference to their parents. But what if John still refuses to participate? Can his parents compel his participation in spite of his dissent? Absolute parental autonomy would empower them to do so. But is this authorization consistent with constrained parental autonomy? That is, does his parents' authorization over his dissent respect his developing and partially actualized personhood?

The answer is yes. To the extent that John's present and future well-being are dependent on his family's well-being, the donation promotes his ends. Children, even competent children, do not have fully developed interests and beliefs, but must be treated with respect to their partially actualized personhood and with respect to their potential to develop into full Kantian persons. To the greatest extent feasible, parents ought to respect their child as a partially actualized person, but John's parents can override his dissent in their endeavour to shape him into the person he is becoming. This is not to deny that his parents' evaluation is made in ignorance of whether he will actually come to hold these values. But parents do not (and should not) merely accept their child's present-day goals and interests as integral components of their child's mature identity. Rather, parents actively shape and steer their child's long-term identity. To this end, John's parents can override his present-day autonomous refusal in order to shape him into the type of person who will come to accept Good Samaritanism and family obligations as integral to his own well-being.[17]

How is John's participation over his dissent respectful of his autonomy? Even if parents can override their child's short-term autonomy to promote his lifetime autonomy, is not his participation as a donor over his competent refusal a threat to both? This answer depends upon the degree and likelihood of the risk to his lifetime autonomy, and the role of the intimate family. A competent child's dissent to a kidney donation for a sibling ought to be binding because of the serious nature of the risks which threaten his short-term and lifetime autonomy. In contrast, the risks and likelihood that a bone marrow donation will threaten John's lifetime autonomy is small, and the risk must be balanced against the potential harm that his refusal can cause his family. John's parents can override John's present-day autonomy to promote family goals because these goals promote John's long-term autonomy even if he doesn't understand this at present. Gaylin explains this as a case where 'is' does not imply 'ought': 'We may deprive the [child] of certain privileges of autonomy out of respect for the person he might become, and out of fear that his own vision of this future may be too limited to allow even himself a proper respect for its value. . . . With the adolescent, we have a right to be concerned about where he is going.'[18] That is, competent children need further guidance. We can restrict their present-day autonomy to promote a richer, fuller, long-term autonomy.

Contrast, then, research that entails a minor increase over minimal risk with no therapeutic benefit (i.e. research which falls under section 46.406 of the Federal Regulations) with a bone marrow donation which has a comparable level of risk. My recommendation in the research setting is that the child's assent is necessary and the child's inability to assent makes the research impermissible to perform. In contrast, parents can authorize a child to serve as a bone marrow donor for a sibling regardless of whether the child can or does assent. The difference is due to the wider autonomy parents are given in balancing the risks and benefits among family members when the risks and benefits accrue within the family in contrast with the stricter standard to which parents are held when balancing the risks and benefits of the child and the larger community.

Cases Summarized

Thus far, I have interpreted the model of constrained parental autonomy to permit parental authorization alone as sufficient to make decisions for children, even competent children, when the decision involves no more than a minor increase over minimal risk. When the decision involves more than a minor increase over minimal risk, there is a threat to the child's basic needs. The model of constrained parental autonomy empowers parents to risk compromising their child's needs for the well-being of the family, but it does not permit them to risk sacrificing their child's *basic* needs. So, when the decision involves more than a minor increase over minimal risk, the competent child's consent is necessary and binding and the incompetent child's participation is impermissible.

I allow parents to override their competent child's dissent in transplants involving no more than a minor increase over minimal risk because to accept a competent child's veto in family decisions when the risks are no more than a slight increase over minimal risk ignores the fact that competent children are not autonomous independent agents, but are dependent members of a family whose long-term goals, values, and beliefs are still somewhat malleable. When the family is intimate, the parents may strive for family goals that would be untenable among strangers without a common purpose or shared group identity. Parents try, and succeed to varying degrees, to instil their own values and beliefs upon their children. At any given moment, a child may not identify fully with her parents' goals and interests, but parents have an obligation not only to promote their child's present interests and identity but also to shape her long-term interests and identity. This obligation does not acutely end once the child has achieved a threshold level of competency.

Children can and do try to influence parental decisions, and respect for the child's competency and growing autonomy requires parents to at least consider their child's request. But when the transplant involves no more than a minor increase over minimal risk, a child's participation without his assent or consent does not necessarily treat him solely as a means. His participation may be consistent with the person he is becoming (or, at least the person his parents would like him to become).

Under the model of constrained parental autonomy, parents have wide discretionary power in making decisions for their incompetent and competent children. Constrained parental autonomy also gives parents wide latitude in deciding how to distribute benefits and risks when the needs and interests of family members conflict or compete for fixed resources. Parental autonomy goes unchallenged, provided that the parents' decisions respect the developing and partially actualized personhood of the child(ren). In decisions that involve no more than a minor increase over minimal risk, parental authority alone is necessary and sufficient (cases I and IV). In decisions that involve more than a minor increase over minimal risk, parents cannot sacrifice their incompetent child's well-being (case II). However, competent children and their parents can consent to the child's participation in activities that involve more than a minor increase over minimal risk, but the veto of either party ought to be binding (case III). These conclusions are summarized in table 6.2. In the next three sections, I will examine additional concerns raised by these conclusions.

TABLE 6.2   *Participation of Children as Organ Donors for Siblings Using the Model of Constrained Parental Autonomy*

Type of Donation	Incompetent Children	Competent Children
Organ donations that entail moderate risks and/or harms	Case I: Donation requires consent by parents alone; child's voice is non-binding	Case IV: Donation requires consent by parents alone; child's voice is non-binding
Organ donations that entail siginificant risks and/or harms	Case II: Donation is impermissible	Case III: Donation requires consent by parents and child; a dissent by either party is binding

3. *Intrafamilial Disagreements*

Constrained parental autonomy is based on the assumption that in intimate families, parents have a conception of the good which they seek to transmit to their children whose well-being they value highly. It is assumed that parents agree on a conception of the good or that they are able to achieve consensus or compromise when their conceptions differ. This requires that their conceptions of the good are not incompatible and that the parents are willing to negotiate disagreements. Although serious disagreements can find their way into, and wreak havoc within, loving families, often such disagreement can be tempered by communication and compromise. The family may involve a neutral third party such as a family counsellor to facilitate dialogue, but ultimately the family members must come to terms with one another. Ideally consensus can be reached; binding external mediation (e.g. from a court) is sought only when more compatible solutions have failed.

The need for binding external mediation implies that the intimate family bonds are ruptured. External mediation does not produce a decision that the family members accept unanimously. Rather, it imposes on the family a course of action to be followed. The aftermath of external mediation in families cannot be compared with similar actions taken in the workplace. Unlike corporations which may be legally forced to accept binding arbitration, the intimate ties that bind families are not necessarily amenable to externally imposed solutions. Families may not be good at or even tolerant of such conflict resolution.[19] Although families can be forced to accept arbitration, they cannot be forced to remain intimate.

Serious tension may develop when a child disagrees with his parents. I argued that if the parents' authorization is consistent with the modified principle of respect, then the parents can override their child's dissent in donations that entail no more than a minor increase over minimal risk. However, the donation takes place in a hospital, where physicians, nurses, or social workers may notice the child's vocal dissent. If they hear the child verbalize his fears or concerns, they may respond to them. They may urge the parents to explore the child's beliefs and to explain their decision in terms that he can understand and accept. Parents cannot demand that the health care personnel ignore their child's vocal dissent. Children are members of other institutions besides the family with whom their parents share authority. For example, a teacher can require that a child sit near a student from another ethnic background despite her parents' prejudiced objection. Likewise, health care personnel can listen to a child's fears about a potential medical procedure. When families find themselves inside the public domain of a hospital, they must realize that other authorities have the freedom to discuss issues which the parents would prefer to be left undiscussed. In fact, respect for children as developing and partially actualized persons requires that health care personnel listen to their viewpoints. The health care personnel may encourage the parents to address their child's dissent.

It is significant that parents require the aid and expertise of health care personnel to harvest their child's organ for transplantation. This point is accentuated if the child refuses to cooperate and physically struggles when the physicians try to bring him to the operating room. Although parents have the right to authorize their child's participation as an organ donor in donations of no more than a minor increase over minimal risk, parents do not have the right to compel physicians to implement this decision. Physicians can refuse to physically restrain the child for non-therapeutic purposes. The parents' need for hospital personnel to restrain their child physically moves the locus of decision making out of the private domain of the family.

If a child is distraught about her parents' decision and is willing to act in such a way as to terminate further parental support and guidance (e.g. she is willing to run away), then her voice cannot be ignored. This is a situation in which the presumption of family intimacy may be misleading. The hospital personnel can require family counselling or submit the case for judicial examination under the statutory requirement of suspected abuse or neglect. The parents cannot claim that the state or the hospital has no right to intervene in a private family decision. The child's willingness to rupture the family bonds moves the decision into the public forum. It could be a grave mistake to allow a child's immature selfishness to override parental autonomy, particularly if there is a good chance that the child will come to regret the decision at a later date. But it could be a more egregious error to ignore the child's dissent if her refusal is due to genuine non-intimacy.[20]

Family counselling may help the parents and child come to

compromise or consensus, but in the end either the parents' or the child's view must prevail. Although society does not compel a competent adult to serve as an organ donor, regardless of the level of risk, parents may compel their child's participation in donations that entail no more than a minor increase over minimal risk. If compulsion requires the aid of physical restraints, further justification is necessary. I believe that such justification may be possible, particularly when the child is incompetent, but I do not advance one here.[21]

4. Bodily Integrity

An alternate argument against my conclusion that parents can override the competent child's refusal to donate when the donation entails less than a minor increase over minimal risk is based on the child's right to bodily integrity. Many policy makers recommend an increase in the child's voice in health care because medical procedures threaten bodily integrity. I do not deny the child's claim that he has a right to bodily integrity, and that forcing him to participate as an organ donor infringes upon this right. But the right to bodily integrity is not absolute: few of these policy makers would be so principled as to deny parents the right to authorize an immunization or nasogastric tube if the child's health were at risk.

The right to bodily integrity is more strictly protected in the impersonal setting than in the intimate setting, not because of implicit consent, but because intimate relationships go beyond the 'rules that govern more impersonal relationships'.[22] While it is always appropriate to demand that one's rights be respected in the public sphere, an appeal to rights ought to be unnecessary in the intimate setting. Within the family, we should resort to rights only if the relationship is irrevocably broken; and even then, we can hope for a more amicable separation.[23] For less serious conflicts, resolution is determined through conversation and compromise. The modified principle of respect for persons does not permit parents to sacrifice one child for the well-being of another, although an individual may suffer setbacks to her particular ends in the pursuit of family goals—setbacks which she would not be expected to accept in a less intimate setting.

A person's right to bodily integrity can be seriously violated by an intimate other (e.g. marital rape). A man who rapes his wife fails to respect her as a person which leaves her with no choice but to resort to her rights. Rights are part of the safety net that prevent personal relationships from concealing injustice indefinitely. Whereas the right to bodily integrity proscribes all unconsented touching by non-intimates, it prohibits only bodily invasions by an intimate that are disrespectful of the other's personhood. If parental authorization of a child's participation as an organ donor is consistent with the modified principle of respect for persons, then parents can compel the child's participation. I have argued that parental authorization of a child to serve as a bone marrow donor which entails a minor increase over minimal risk is consistent with respect for his personhood even if the child dissents. However, parents cannot compel their child to serve as a kidney donor, which entails more than a minor increase over minimal risk, without the child's consent. The child and the parents must consent to donations that entail more than a minor increase over minimal risk in order that these donations be consistent with the modified principle of respect for persons.

5. *Expanding Donations by Children Beyond the Family*

I have assumed throughout this chapter that the child donor is to serve as a donor for a sibling.[24] I believe that the arguments presented cannot be widened to allow a child to serve as an organ donor for a stranger. The role of the child as an organ donor for an intrafamilial transplant is justified in part because the intrafamilial donation not only uses the child as a means to help another family member, but it also serves to promote the family's well-being, on which the child's own well-being depends. Restricting children's donations to other family members acknowledges the *intimate* interconnection between the child's and the family's well-being that is not mirrored in the more impersonal relationship of the child to society at large.[25]

Can I expand my position to allow children to serve as organ donors for other intimate individuals (e.g. close family friends)? There is one important empirical difference: histocompatibility is proportionately related to blood lineage, so that friends are often not histocompatible.[26] (To the extent that our friends are of similar racial, ethnic, and religious backgrounds, we may be more histocompatible with a friend than with a stranger, but probably not enough to make a difference especially with the newest generation of immunosuppressive drugs.) Thus, there is little advantage in having a child rather than one of her parents serve as an organ donor for a friend.

Imagine, however, a scenario where organ size is an issue:[27] Can children serve as organ donors for intimate individuals outside the family? I believe that the arguments regarding intimate relationships can be extrapolated to permit donations between children and close family friends.[28] However, I propose that extrafamilial donations undergo judicial review, in contrast with my position that intrafamilial donations should not be subject to routine review. The difference is that families are intimate groups which have a presumptive right to non-interference by the state. Judicial review of extrafamilial donations is important from the standpoint of social justice; we must be wary of any trend which supports the utilization of children as organ donors in favour of adults, even if the procedure incurs only minimal harm. Children are vulnerable because of their immaturity and dependent status. Well-meaning but misguided guardians (as well as immoral guardians) may exploit them. A policy which requires judicial review for cases involving child donations to intimate others beyond the nuclear family reduces the risk of exploitation.

6. Conclusion

According to the model of constrained parental autonomy, parents should have wide autonomy in deciding whether their child participates as an intrafamilial organ donor. In donations that entail no more than a minor increase over minimal risk, parental authorization alone is sufficient, regardless of whether the child is competent and regardless of whether the child assents or dissents to the proposed bodily intrusion. However, when the donation entails more than a minor increase over minimal risk, parental autonomy is constrained by the modified principle of respect.

Incompetent children are prohibited from participating as donors and competent children can participate only if they and their parents consent.

Notes

1. Whether the first live kidney donors should have been children is a significant but moot point. The National Commission for the Protection of Human Subjects of Biomedical and Behavioral Research for the conduct of research involving children recommends that, when possible, experimentation should first be performed on animals and adult humans before proceeding to experimentation on children. National Commission for the Protection of Human Subjects of Biomedical and Behavioral Research, *Report and Recommendations: Research Involving Children* (Washington, DC: U.S. Printing Office, September, 1977), 2–3. If these recommendations are applied to live transplant donors (and they should be), then they would require, when possible, that adults serve as live donors in innovative transplants before children.

2. Foster v. Harrison, Eq. No. 68674 (Mass., November 20, 1957); Huskey v. Harrison, Eq. No. 68666 (Mass., August 30, 1957); and Masden v. Harrison, Eq. No. 68651 (Mass., June 12, 1957).

3. The problem with this approach is that it requires judicial authorization for all transplants in which children are involved. I do not believe this is necessary for intrafamilial donations. It permits too much state supervision and intervention in family decisions that are appropriately made privately. Contrast sections 2 and 5 below.

4. The Court's finding that kidney donations are donations of minimal risk is mistaken, as I discuss later in this chapter in notes 10–12 and accompanying text.

5. Whether kidney donations serve the best interest of the child is speculative at best. Participation as an organ donor is not undertaken to serve the donor child's physical well-being. Whether the non-physical benefits outweigh the harms, risks and costs depend on how one measures each factor. Different families will weigh these factors differently. Given my arguments that intimate families should not be held to a best interest standard when making decisions for children, the issue is moot. Instead, I use the modified principle of respect as the guidance principle.

6. *Masden v. Harrison*, 4.

7. When the courts have rejected the participation of a child as an organ

donor, they have based their decision on the best interest standard as well. Consider, for example, *In re Richardson*, in which the court held that a kidney donation was inconsistent with the child's best interest (284 So.2d. 185 La. App. (1973)).

8. Nathan v. Farinelli, Eq. No. 74–87 (Mass., July 3, 1974).

9. The question of who are the appropriate decision makers to determine whether a child should participate as an organ recipient was never addressed by the courts. An ethical argument using the modified principle of respect would assign this role solely to the parents, regardless of whether the transplant is experimental or non-experimental. If the transplant is classified as experimental therapy, then the transplant is research that offers the child a direct benefit. I argued in Chapter 5.8A that parents should be the sole decision makers for therapeutic research. If the transplant is non-experimental therapy, then it classifies as therapeutic medical care, which I discuss in Chapter 7. There, again, I argue that parents should be the sole decision makers.

10. The exact risk is unknown. Overall, the risk of anaesthesia is often cited as less than a 1 in 10,000 chance of suffering any significant morbidity or mortality (from general anaesthesia). The actual risk for potential organ donors is even less because organ donors are a healthy population, in contrast with the average patient who undergoes anaesthesia. Although the exact risk for a healthy paediatric patient is not available, the risk of mortality for undergoing general anaesthesia in *healthy adult subjects*, for example, is approximately 1 in 339,450. See D. Brown (ed.), *Risk and Outcome in Anesthesia*, 2nd ed. (Philadelphia, Pa.: J. B. Lipincott, 1992), 15.

11. For example, Dunn et al. cite major peri-operative complications at 7 per cent. See J. F. Dunn, 'Living Related Kidney Donors: A 14-Year Experience', *Annals of Surgery*, 203 (1986), 637–42. Najarian et al. surveyed all members of the American Society of Transplant Surgeons about donor mortality and documented seventeen peri-operative deaths after live kidney donation. They calculated the peri-operative mortality to be about 0.03 per cent. J. S. Najarian, B. M. Chavers, L. E. McHugh, and A. J. Matas, '20 Years or More of Follow-up of Living Kidney Donors', *Lancet*, 340 (8823) (1992), 807–10.

12. Dunn et al. cite major late complications at 20 per cent (Dunn et al., 'Living Related'). Some of his data are contestable. He reports 5.6 per cent with definite hypertension, but other studies have shown that donors are no more likely to become hypertensive than their siblings. See, for example, R. M. Hakim, R. C. Goldszer, and B. M. Brenner, 'Hypertension and Proteinuria: Long-Term Sequellae of Uninephrectomy in Humans', *Kidney International*, 25 (1984), 930–6, and Najarian et al. '20 Years or More').

The risks and harms associated with allowing a child to be an organ donor may be easier to understand if they are compared to the risks and harms that children encounter daily. The risks and harms of allowing a child to participate as a blood donor, for example, are comparable to the risks and harms of allowing a child to play tag in the schoolyard. Serving as a bone marrow donor entails greater risks and harms on the scale of playing interscholastic American football. And the risks and harms of allowing a child to serve as a kidney donor are comparable to the risks and harms of allowing a child to learn how to drive a car. It is helpful to keep these risks and harms in perspective as I consider whether parents ought to have the authority to authorize their child's participation as an organ donor.

13. In this chapter, I do not distinguish between the child who is unable to assent from the incompetent child who can assent but cannot give informed consent. Both classes of children are incompetent and my conclusions are the same. This differs from my arguments in Chapter 5. The difference is because the benefits and risks of intrafamilial organ donations accrue within the family.

14. One could also argue that Ann is being treated as the developing person that she is because it is assumed that she would consent if she could. I reject this line of argument because I do not believe that presumed consent protects children. Ramsey explains why presumed consent is inadequate in P. Ramsey, 'The Enforcement of Morals: Nontherapeutic Research on Children', *Hastings Center Report*, 6 (1976), 21–30.

15. Of great concern is whether a child can actually refuse to participate if her parents are encouraging her to participate. This problem, however, is not unique to competent children. Fellner and Marshall interviewed twenty adult kidney donors and ten potential kidney donors. They found that all of the donors made their decisions impulsively, prior to consulting their spouses, and none revoked their initial consent after consulting with the transplant team. Given the process by which potential donors made their decision, Fellner and Marshall concluded that living adult donors do not give *informed* consent. They argue that living donors should not be used in organ transplantation. C. Fellner and J. Marshall, 'Kidney Donors: The Myth of Informed Consent', *American Journal of Psychiatry*, 126 (1970), 1247–50.

These findings are not surprising, given that potential donors are usually intimate family members, with whom the recipient's identity and goals are interwoven. I believe that a universal prohibition of all living related kidney donors would be inconsistent with a wide range of conceptions of what the good life entails. Contrary to Fellner and Marshall, I believe we must accept the competent family member's consent as valid, even if the consent does not stand up to the strictest standards of voluntariness.

16. See Chapter 5.7.
17. If John does not come to accept these values as his own, then he may argue, in retrospect, that he was treated as a mere means. He may also argue that since no adult is ever forced to be an organ donor for another—see, for example, Shimp v. McFall (10 Pa. D. & C.3d 90 (C.P. Ct. 1978))—that his participation should have required his consent.

    These arguments are misguided as they ignore the role of the intimate family in decision making for children. Constrained parental autonomy permits wide parental latitude in how parents treat their children, compared with what adults (even intimate adults) can require of each other. John's parents can compromise his 'best' interest to promote family goals. Ideally, John would share in these goals, but if he does not, his parents are the final arbiters in intrafamilial disputes and they can override his competent dissent. Adults, on the other hand, are the final arbiters of their own actions. Adults have the right to decide whether or not to compromise (even sacrifice) their own interests for the well-being of the family. This does not mean that family members cannot try to change the decisions made by adult members, only that ultimately the competent adult's dissent is legally determinative.

18. W. Gaylin, 'Competence: No Longer All or None', in W. Gaylin and R. Macklin (eds.), *Who Speaks for the Child: The Problems of Proxy Consent* (New York: Plenum Press, 1982), 53.
19. I thank Leslie Moore for pressing me on this point.
20. For example, it may be revealed during mediation that the child refuses to be a donor because her sibling has repeatedly raped her and her parents have refused to protect her. I thank Dave Schmidtz for this example.
21. Although I do not address these issues in Chapter 5, these and related concerns apply there as well. In fact, verbal or physical resistance in the research setting should raise large red flags, particularly when the research is non-therapeutic.
22. J. Hardwig, 'Should Women Think in Terms of Rights?', *Ethics*, 97 (1987), as reprinted by C. R. Sunstein (ed.), in *Feminism and Political Theory* (Chicago, Ill.: University of Chicago Press, 1990), 57.
23. See, for example, A. Baier, 'Trusting Ex-intimates', in G. Graham and H. LaFollette (eds.), *Person to Person* (Philadelphia, Pa.: Temple University Press, 1989), 269–81.
24. Although there may be additional conflicts of interests, I believe but

do not argue for the position that these same arguments could be used to justify the child's role as a donor for a parent.

25. Rather, acting as a donor to a stranger is similar to serving as a subject of human experimentation, in that the rewards are more diffuse. I explored when children can participate as subjects of human experimentation in Chapter 5.

26. Histocompatibility refers to the compatibility (similarity) of the donor and the recipient's immunologic status. Organs are classified by HLA-antigens. There are four major classes of antigens. Children get half of their antigens from each parent so children will match 50 per cent of their antigens with each parent. There is a 25 per cent chance of siblings being HLA-identical. Identical twins have identical HLA-antigens and so a twin will accept an organ donated from his twin brother without the need for immunosuppressive therapy. During the early transplant era, when immunosuppressive therapy to combat rejection was less effective, transplants were done only on identical twins because all the other transplanted organs were quickly rejected. Today, immunosuppressive therapy is so successful that many transplants can be done despite the lack of histocompatibility between donor and recipient. However, immunosuppressants have drawbacks; individuals who take immunosuppressants are at serious risk for life-threatening infections and for secondary cancers.

27. This scenario is becoming less frequent with the ability to use segments of living and cadaveric adult organs for paediatric transplantation. See, for example, H. Bismuth and D. Houssin, 'Reduced-Sized Orthotopic Liver Graft in Hepatic Transplantation in Children', *Surgery*, 95 (1984), 367–70; C. E. Broelsch et al., 'Liver Transplantation Including the Concept of Reduced-Size Liver Transplants in Children', *Annals of Surgery*, 208 (1988), 410–20; and E. M. Alonso et al., ' "Split-Liver" Orthotopic Liver Transplantation (OLT)', *Pediatric Research*, 25 (1989), 107A, Abstract.

28. There is a renewed interest in the ethics of friendship relationships. See, for example, N. K. Badhwar (ed.), *Friendship: A Philosophical Reader* (Ithaca, NY: Cornell University Press, 1993); and M. Friedman, *What Are Friends For?* (Ithaca, NY: Cornell University Press, 1993). Many of the authors argue that friends, like family members, incur special obligations that are not owed to strangers. One limitation of these essays is that they discuss relationships between adult friends, and very little is written on the friendship relationship between children or between children and adults

7

The Child as Patient

1. *Non-Experimental Therapeutic Decision Making*

Most of the medical care which children receive from physicians is not experimental. Non-experimental medical care includes preventive health care (e.g. immunizations), the treatment of acute illnesses or injuries, and the treatment of chronic conditions. The care may be sought electively or emergently; and the treatment may serve to prevent disability, to enhance quality of life, to alleviate pain, or to treat life-threatening conditions. The care can be obtained in a private physician's office, a walk-in clinic, or in the hospital setting. Almost always, the intention of the practitioner, child, and parents have a convergent focus: the child's medical well-being.[1]

Most non-experimental therapeutic medical treatment, like most research, involves some risks and uncertainty. In general, however, the risks and benefits are better known and post-marketing surveillance frequently has confirmed long-term safety and efficacy. In Chapter 5, I argued that when research offers the prospect of direct therapeutic benefit to the potential child subject, parents should have final decision-making authority as to whether their child participates. I argued that the parents' decision was both necessary and sufficient for *all* children, even competent children. This conclusion was not meant to advocate excluding children, particularly competent children, from the decision-making process, but only to acknowledge that parents have final decision-making authority when research offers a *direct* therapeutic benefit. If these arguments are valid for therapeutic research, then they are even more convincing with respect to non-experimental therapy. In this chapter, I explore whether the non-experimental nature of this treatment permits more or less parental flexibility in authorizing or refusing to authorize treatment, and whether it influences the appropriate role for state intervention.

2. *Parental Refusals*

Consider the following two cases. In the first case, Paul Jones is a three-year-old with acute lymphocytic leukaemia (ALL). His oncologist offers two medical options: chemotherapy alone or chemotherapy in conjunction with cerebral radiation therapy (XRT).[2] The advantage of cerebral XRT is that it reduces the risk of recurrence. However, cerebral XRT in children is associated with various degrees of learning disabilities and growth deficiency. Statistically, the addition of XRT results in a lower probability of mortality, but a higher probability of morbidity. In either case, if the cancer recurs, cure is still likely. Paul's parents, in good faith, can choose either course depending on how they balance the risks, benefits, and long-term prognoses. Some parents may seek greater security in cure; others may be more concerned with quality of life. Some parents may be risk-averse; others may be unperturbed by uncertainty. In the abstract, neither regimen is better than the other; both decisions are consistent with 'standard medical care'. Because reasonable persons disagree as to which of the two options is preferable, either decision is respected.

What if the Joneses decide against chemotherapy or chemotherapy plus XRT for Paul, and request laetrile and megavitamins instead? The Joneses reject chemotherapy because they are distressed at using poisons to treat their son's ailment, and they find a holistic health care consultant who recommends laetrile and megavitamins. Although the oncologist argues that this treatment is ineffective, the holistic advisor claims otherwise.[3] The Joneses decide to pursue the homoeopathic alternative. What should the oncologist do?

Contrast the case of Paul Jones with the case of Ann Miller, a fifteen-year-old with a sore throat. Her pain began at dinner time. At midnight she has a high fever and is unable to sleep. Mrs Miller takes Ann to the local emergency room where a quick-strep is positive.[4] The physician offers Ann and Mrs Miller two options: a ten-day course of oral penicillin which needs to be taken three times a day, or a shot of penicillin. He explains that neither will improve

Ann's symptoms this evening. The advantage of the shot is that it is a one-time dose and Ann will be assured of appropriate treatment to prevent acute rheumatic fever and rheumatic heart disease, the most serious sequelae of untreated strep infections. Issues to be weighed include efficacy, cost, convenience, attendant risks, and compliance. For example, a physician may advocate the injection to ensure compliance, particularly if the child has an underlying immunodeficiency. The parent may choose one route for pragmatic reasons such as convenience or cost. The child may also have a preference. She may detest the taste of the antibiotic and would prefer to get a shot, or she may fear needles and promise to comply with taking the medicine.

Either course of treatment is consistent with respect for Ann's partially actualized and developing personhood. According to the model of constrained parental autonomy, Mrs Miller's decision should be decisive, even if Ann dissents to the particular therapeutic modality, because parents are the final arbiter in intrafamilial disputes. Let us suppose that Mrs Miller prefers an injection because she believes that Ann will be poorly compliant once the symptoms are gone. However, in this instance, Ann convinces her mother to get a prescription for pills. The pharmacies are closed and the emergency room does not have any samples. The physician explains that there is no danger in waiting twelve hours, even several days. He advises Ann to take some Tylenol, and tells Ann's mother to fill the prescription in the morning. By morning Ann feels fine. She has no fever and her appetite is normal, which is not typical of Ann when she has strep throat. She asks to go to school. Given Ann's quick recovery, Mrs Miller decides that her sore throat was probably not a strep infection, and she does not fill the prescription.[5] Is Mrs Miller's action consistent with the modified principle of respect?

The fact is that Ann may or may not have strep throat. The quick-strep test cannot differentiate between an acute infection and a carrier state in which the patient carries certain strains of strep on her tonsils, but they are not the causative agent of her symptoms. Most children with strep throat feel better in two or three days with or without treatment. The reason to take the antibiotics is not to relieve the pain, but to prevent the possible sequela of acute rheumatic fever and/or rheumatic heart disease.

The conservative response is to ask, Why take the risk,

particularly since a course of penicillin costs less than ten dollars? In part, the response is that penicillin is not totally benign. It may cause a yeast infection, decrease the effectiveness of oral contraceptives, or induce a serious allergic reaction. There is a high likelihood that Mrs Miller's decision to forgo the penicillin will not cause serious sequelae, and may, in some circumstance, prevent some untoward events. And yet, virtually all physicians and epidemiologists will agree that the benefits outweigh the risks which is why penicillin is 'standard medical care' for strep throat in children.

Contrast this calculation with the calculation necessary to determine whether to authorize a child's participation in therapeutic research when it is unknown whether the benefits outweigh the risks and costs. The experimental nature of the treatment indicates that there is no expert consensus on whether participation is medically beneficial. Given the uncertainty, parental autonomy to authorize or to refuse to authorize such treatment is respected. But when the benefits are proven, and the treatment is judged by the medical community to be 'medically indicated', then parental autonomy can be constrained.[6]

Are the decisions by the Joneses and Mrs Miller to ignore medical advice and standard medical care consistent with respect for their children's partially actualized and developing personhood? With laetrile and megavitamins alone, Paul will almost certainly die, whereas he has a greater than 50 per cent chance of survival with chemotherapy (with or without XRT).[7] As such, the Joneses' decision is medically neglectful. In contrast, the consequences of not taking penicillin are most likely benign. According to the modified principle of respect, an action is respectful of the person based on intentions and principles, and not on whether particular consequences are good. Both decisions are medically neglectful.

Cases of parental medical neglect range from inappropriate to life-threatening. Since the Joneses' decision is life-threatening, and treatment has a high probability of cure, Paul's oncologist will likely seek and obtain a court order to treat Paul over his parents' dissent.[8] The courts are quick to give court orders, particularly when the treatment is life-saving, although they will intervene in some quality-of-life decisions as well.[9] Mrs Miller's decision to forgo filling her daughter's prescription, although inappropriate, will most likely go unnoticed. Ann will not resurface for medical attention unless she develops acute rheumatic fever or until another acute illness strikes. Given the low probability of medical complications from the decision, both the effort and coercion necessary to enforce compliance is not worth the cost. At minimum, it would require that the state supervise pharmacy records to ensure that all prescriptions are filled. To ensure full compliance would further require state attendance for each dose, or less accurately, a random drug cabinet search to count the pills that have not been taken. Both are overly intrusive and impractical, given the fact that Ann will most likely do well, even if she does not get the medicine.

Although the consequences should not determine whether a decision is consistent with the modified principle of respect, the predicted consequences should influence when intervention is appropriate. When standard treatment has a high cure rate, and denial of treatment will most likely result in an untimely death, state intervention is justified. When the probability of serious morbidity and mortality is low, state intervention should rarely be sought.[10] The cases of Paul Jones and Ann Miller reflect opposite ends of the spectrum. In the next section, I will consider what criteria should justify state intervention regarding less clear-cut examples.

3. *Parental Refusals and the Role for State Intervention*

When parents make decisions which are contrary to their child's basic interests,[11] the state, as *parens patriae*, has the right to intervene. However the state must balance this power with its limitations. The state should not be eager to intervene in the intimate family because it is unqualified to make the myriad of daily subjective decisions for a child that may follow disruption, particularly if the child is removed from parental custody. The state cannot offer the intimacy, stability, and emotional bonds that exist in a family which are essential for the normal physical and psychological growth and well-being of children. In general, the state's goals are better served by deferring to parental autonomy. And this deference is often a self-fulfilling prophecy; the presumption of parental autonomy is often enough to motivate parents to promote their child's *basic needs*, if not their child's *best interest*.

When the state intervenes because parents are neglectful or abusive, the state's intervention should be less detrimental than lack of state intervention (i.e. 'the least detrimental alternative').[12] Joseph Goldstein, Anna Freud, and Albert Solnit propose three criteria to be met in order for the state to justify intervention: '(1) Medical experts agree that treatment is non-experimental and appropriate for the child, (2) denial of that treatment would result in death, and (3) the anticipated result of treatment is what society would want for every child—a chance for normal healthy growth or a life worth living.'[13] The three criteria appropriately seek to limit state intervention. In what follows I will explicate and revise the criteria.

The first criterion suggests the need for agreement by medical experts and not among the health care community at large. The distinction is important. Consider, for example, a child with cancer that is highly curable with chemotherapy but whose parents find a physician who believes in the efficacy of laetrile. In 1979, such a case came before the New York Court of Appeals. Joseph Hofbauer was a three-year-old whose physician, a cancer specialist, recommended chemotherapy. His parents found a physician who did not specialize in cancer who advocated nutritional and metabolic therapy including laetrile for cancer. When they stopped Joseph's chemotherapy, they were charged with neglect. The court found the Hofbauers were not neglectful because they had entrusted their child's care to a physician: '[G]reat deference must be accorded a parent's choice as to the mode of medical treatment to be undertaken and the physician selected to administer the same.'[14]

Other courts, however, have taken notice of the care givers' credentials. In *Custody of a minor*, the Superior Judicial Court of Massachusetts found against the parents of Chad Green, a three-year-old with leukaemia, and the court's ruling was upheld by the Superior Judicial Council of Massachusetts. Although the Greens found four expert witnesses to support laetrile and megavitamins, the court noted that none practised in Massachusetts and none claimed expertise in haematology or oncology. The court rejected their medical testimony.[15]

These cases illustrate the importance of distinguishing

between medical experts and any health care provider. Had this criterion been adhered to by the courts, both the Hofbauers and the Greens would have been found neglectful, despite the testimony of a few unconventional health care providers.

The second criterion proposed by Goldstein, Freud, and Solnit permits state intervention only if denial of the treatment would result in death. Furthermore, they restrict state intervention to those life-or-death situations in which there are proven treatments with a high probability of success.[16] This is insufficient because it does not permit state intervention if the denial of care would result in serious setbacks to a child's *basic needs*.[17]

The following hypothetical cases, described by Wesley Sokolosky, explain why the second criterion needs revision.[18] Twin infants feed poorly and have problems digesting regular formula. A work-up reveals that one twin was born with phenylketonuria (PKU) and the other with galactosemia, two inborn errors of metabolism. Dietary management of each disease is very successful. If untreated, PKU leads to mental retardation and seizures but not death, whereas galactosemia results in hepatic damage, mental retardation, cataracts, and eventually death. Following Goldstein, Freud, and Solnit's second criterion, the state would be able to override the parents' refusal to follow the therapeutic diet for the child with galactosemia only and not for the child with PKU because only the former results in death.[19] Sokolosky agrees with Goldstein and colleagues' main thrust to respect parental autonomy, but he recommends allowing state intervention not only to save the child's life but also if the state's treatment is 'substantially preferable'.[20] Sokolosky compares the consequences (weighted for both likelihood and desirability) of each of the alternate treatments, and favours the decision which is *most* beneficial to the child.[21]

Sokolosky is correct to find the second criterion too limited, but his solution holds parents to a best interest standard. My suggestion would be to modify the second criterion to require state intervention in those cases in which denial of medical treatment would cause any of the child's basic needs to fall below a certain threshold. None of a child's basic needs can be sacrificed for other needs that the child or other family members have. If parents fulfil their child's basic needs, then their decision is consistent with the modified principle of respect and that is all that should be required of them. Beyond this threshold, parents should be free to balance their child's other needs and interests with those of other family members and of the whole family. This means that parents do not have to choose medical treatments which maximize their child's medical well-being, only that their decision must satisfy some threshold level of medical need. Even this may be too stringent as there may be some children who can never attain this threshold, regardless of the amount of resources allocated to them. Goldstein, Freud, and Solnit suggest limiting state intervention to cases in which there is a therapeutic treatment which has proven efficacy and a high likelihood of success[22] (i.e. to cases in which it is highly likely that the child can achieve a threshold level of a primary good with a reasonable resource allotment). I accept these qualifications as families and communities cannot be expected to exhaust all of their funds in the pursuit of one child's primary good.

The third criterion is the most controversial, as it involves quality-of-life judgements. Goldstein, Freud, and Solnit argue for broad deference to parents:

Those cases in which reasonable and responsible persons can and do disagree about whether the 'life' after treatment will be 'worth living' or 'normal' and thus about what is 'right' are precisely those in which parents must remain free of coercive state intervention in deciding whether to reject or consent to the medical program offered to their child.[23]

Goldstein, Freud, and Solnit claim that parents should be given broad autonomy as they are the ones who will have to live with the decision. They cite Raymond Duff, a neonatologist, who also held that quality-of-life decisions should be made by the parents in consultation with their physician:

Families know their values, priorities and resources better than anyone else. Presumably they, with the doctor, can make the better choice as a private affair. Certainly, they, more than anyone else, must live with the consequences. . . . If they cannot cope adequately with the child and their other responsibilities and survive as a family, they may feel that the death option is a forced choice. . . . But that is not necessarily bad, and who knows of a better way?[24]

That is, Goldstein, Freud, and Solnit believe that parents should have the autonomy to decide whether a life-saving treatment should be performed on their child, not solely on the basis of whether the treatment is likely to be effective, but on the basis of whether they believe that the resultant life will be 'worth living'. The presumption of parental autonomy in health care decision making, buttressed by the right to family privacy, should leave controversial quality-of-life cases as a family matter that is not subject to state scrutiny.

The problem with their criterion is that it allows parents to determine what a life worth living is, from their own perspective, or from the perspective of the family, without regard to whether the life is worth living from the perspective of the child. The difference is obvious. Consider, for example, the case of Baby Doe, an infant born with Down syndrome and a duodenal atresia (a malformation of the gastrointestinal [GI] tract which is easily corrected with surgery). The parents refused to consent to surgery and refused intravenous nutrition, which meant that the child would die from starvation. The hospital unsuccessfully sought a court order to force treatment and Baby Doe died untreated. According to Goldstein, Freud, and Solnit's criterion, the parents' decision should have been respected.

In a review of the case, the government noted that the goal of the proposed abdominal surgery was to treat the GI obstruction and that the surgery would have achieved that goal. It also noted that if the child had been born with normal chromosomes, refusal of surgery would never have been tolerated. So the parents and physicians were making a quality-of-life judgement that Down syndrome in and of itself leads to a life not worth living. The government responded that many persons with trisomy 21 lead happy lives and that to withhold the surgery neglected the *basic* health needs of the child. The government classified this decision as neglectful, and banned such decisions.[25]

The Does' decision was not atypical in the early 1980s. The state, however, intervened because the Does' refusal to authorize surgery threatened their child's basic medical needs. When parents (either well-meaning or neglectful) make neglectful decisions, their decisions must be overridden. In general, the state takes custody of the child to authorize the treatment, and then the child is returned to parental custody. Not all parents accept this solution. Some continue to reject the child and place the child for adoption. Families cannot be forced to be intimate, but this does not empower families to impede the fulfilment of any basic needs of any of their children members.

This is not to say that parents must always elect to preserve life. Parents can refuse treatment for their child if life itself is a burden for the child, offers no benefit to the child from the child's own perspective, or will not promote the child's personhood. Parents may even be obligated to refuse treatment if the burden of the treatment is greatly outweighed by any potential benefits; for example, cardiopulmonary resuscitation for a terminally ill child who has intractable pain. As such, I would revise the third criterion to read that state intervention should be sought only in those cases in which the anticipated result of treatment promotes the child's personhood or at least gives the child a chance for a life worth living as evaluated from the child's own perspective (regardless of what a parent would want for him or herself).

In summary, I would revise the Goldstein, Freud, and Solnit criteria to read:

> State intervention in medical care should be limited to those cases in which (1) medical experts agree that the treatment is non-experimental and appropriate for the child; (2) denial of the treatment (which is of proven efficacy and has a high probability of success) would result in the deprivation of the child's basic needs; and (3) the anticipated result of treatment gives the child a chance for normal healthy growth or a life worth living as evaluated from the child's own perspective.

These criteria require parents to authorize treatment that is consistent with standard medical care, and require state intervention if parents fail to authorize such care. On first blush, this suggests that parental autonomy is respected only when parents make the medically appropriate choice. More accurately, respect for parental autonomy is shown by giving parents the prima facie right to determine what is appropriate medical care for their child, all things considered. The state often respects parental authorizations and refusals, although parental authority is not absolute. Parents share responsibility for the upbringing and well-being of their children with other authorities in the community. When parental decisions appear to be contrary to their child's basic needs, or when parents define their ideal vision of the community to exclude their disabled child, then the state, as *parens patriae*, must intervene.

A decision to override parental autonomy should not be made casually. When treatment is not an emergency, parents can demand a thorough review of the state's decision to override their decision before court-ordered medical care is given. The courts should evaluate the following conditions: the certainty of the diagnosis and prognosis, the probability of success with the treatment, the probability of failure without the treatment, and the invasiveness of state intervention. The state's mandate to intervene increases when there is a high certainty in diagnosis, the treatment has a high likelihood of cure, and when the denial of treatment is likely to harm the child's developing personhood.[26]

4. *Parental Demands for Treatment*

The traditional example regarding the limits to patient and surrogate autonomy is when the patient or his surrogate demands *futile* treatment. The problem is determining when treatment is futile. Consider, for example, Rose, a fifty-year-old woman, the mother of two grown children, who has terminal bone cancer and is in considerable pain, some of which cannot be relieved by medication. She is competent to make treatment decisions for herself. As a competent patient, she can refuse treatment, even life-sustaining treatment. But what if Rose wants cardiopulmonary resuscitation (CPR) in the event that her heart and lungs fail? Can her physician argue that since she is dying, CPR is futile? CPR will not reverse her underlying illness although it may prolong her life by several days or weeks. If Rose wants time to get her estate in order, to live to see her first grandchild, or to say goodbye to relatives who live out of state, CPR serves a valid, albeit temporary function: it prolongs life for a patient who wants it prolonged.[27] For another patient in the same condition, CPR may not serve a valid purpose. For him, CPR would only prolong his dying. What one patient defines as futile or too painful, another may choose to undergo. One patient sees CPR as prolonging death, the other as prolonging life. Thus, futility appears to be a value-laden notion which depends on who defines it and by what criteria.

This is not an obvious conclusion. There is wide divergence about what constitutes futile care, in part because there is no agreed-upon definition of what constitutes futility.[28] Physiological futility is treatment that cannot restore cardiovascular or respiratory function,[29] but most definitions of futility go further. They include cases in which there are low probabilities of survival, or poor quality-of-life judgements. But each of these factors entails a value judgement as to what extent an individual is willing to undergo a painful procedure that has negligible survival odds. Whether an individual is willing to undergo a procedure that may prolong his life but has a significant risk of leaving him permanently unconscious is a personal decision that depends upon the particular values that an individual holds.

Whose values, then, should the definition of futility incorporate: the values of the individual patient, the physician, or the community at large? Or is the whole notion of futility question-begging? Isn't the fifty-year-old with metastatic bone cancer who refuses CPR really saying, 'Given my quality of life, prolonging my life is not worth the burdens and costs'? By contrast, isn't the other patient with the same condition who demands CPR really saying, 'I value my life, regardless of its quality'? Treatments that are labelled 'futile' that are not physiologically futile actually describe a low-probability, low-efficacy, or poor quality-of-life judgement. If futility is just a quality-of-life judgement, only the patient's (or his surrogates') values should be weighed.[30]

When the patient is a child, the parents are and ought to be the surrogate decision makers. Parents must authorize life-saving treatment if it is a proven treatment which has a high probability of success. If they do not, the state, as *parens patriae*, must authorize such treatment. However, when the treatment has a low probability of success, is likely to result in a poor quality of life, or is experimental, the parents are free to decide whether the benefits outweigh the risks and costs. It is a value-laden, quality-of-life decision that should be theirs to make.[31]

The question remains whether there comes a point when physicians should override patient or surrogate decisions because the likelihood of benefit is so low or the potential benefit can yield only a very poor quality of life;[32] that is, when a treatment is both 'virtually futile and inhumane'.[33] Even if the treatment can achieve some physiologic goals, the pains, harms and costs to the patient prohibit parents morally from authorizing treatment because the treatment is not consistent with the modified principle of respect. The case of Baby L as described in the *New England Journal of Medicine* is potentially such a case. I quote the case at length to show why I believe this case illustrates inhumane treatment.

The Case of Baby L

The patient, a two-year-old girl, was born at 36 weeks, weighing 1970 g to a 33-year-old mother who had been pregnant three times before and had given birth to three live infants. The pregnancy was complicated by fetal hydronephrosis and oligohydramnios in the last trimester. Decelerations in the fetal heart rate and thick meconium below the vocal cords were noted at delivery. Apgar scores were 1 at 1 minute, 4 at 5 minutes, and 5 at 10 minutes. The infant was resuscitated, stabilized, and weaned from mechanical ventilation. Over a period of weeks the infant's respiratory function improved, but the neurologic condition remained very depressed, with no responsiveness except to pain.

The infant underwent a gastrostomy at the age of one month, a Nissen fundoplication at four months, and a tracheostomy at seven months. There were intermittent episodes of aspiration and uncontrolled seizures. She was discharged after 14 months with 24-hour nursing care, but was readmitted within two weeks for recurrent pneumonia. During the next several months she was repeatedly hospitalized for pneumonia and septic shock. At the age of 23 months the child—having been readmitted with worsening pneumonia and sepsis—required mechanical ventilation and cardiovascular support. During those 23 months of recurrent pneumonia and four cardiopulmonary arrests, the mother had continued to demand that everything possible be done to ensure the child's survival.

A meeting of the chiefs of service, primary care physicians, nurses, hospital counsel, and chairpersons of the institutional ethics committee was convened to discuss the advisability of reinstituting mechanical ventilation and cardiovascular support. Given a child with such extensive neurological deficits that she could experience only pain, they agreed unanimously that further medical intervention was not in the best interests of the patient. In their opinion, further intervention would subject the child to additional pain without affecting the underlying condition or ultimate outcome. The child's mother rejected that opinion.[34]

In an unprecedented move, the hospital attorneys decided to go to court. The issue that they wanted decided was, 'What should be done when a parent demands treatment that the physician and other care givers believe to be against the best interests of the child?'[35] The case, however, was not adjudicated because a paediatric neurologist from another institution was willing to accommodate the parent's wishes and the child was transferred. In 1990, Baby L was four years old. Her medical update read: 'She remains blind, deaf and quadriplegic and is fed through the gastrostomy. She averages a seizure a day. Her pulmonary status has improved, but she continues to require intensive home nursing 16 hours a day. Her mental status remains that of a three-month-old infant.'[36]

I wish the case had been litigated. The question that I would want the court to address is not 'What should be done when a parent demands treatment that the physicians and other care givers believe to be against the *best interest* of the child?' but rather 'What should be done when a parent demands treatment that the physicians and other care givers believe to be virtually futile and inhumane?' I do not believe we can or should hold parents to a best-interest-of-the-child standard, but what if the mother's actions are contrary to the modified principle of respect?

The authors claim that the physicians decided to refuse to perform further treatment 'based on the team's assessment that unless a reversal or amelioration of the underlying condition could be expected, painful interventions would be futile and inhumane'.[37] Depending on one's criteria for futility, the treatment was not futile. The mechanical ventilation cannot be defined as strictly (physiologically) futile because it did prolong Baby L's existence. What the authors meant is that the treatment is virtually futile because the respirator did not prolong what they perceived to be meaningful life.

The report states that the treatment was inhumane because Baby L cannot experience pleasure but can experience pain. As such, her only goal can be the absence of pain. As long as Baby L's existence causes her no pain, medical personnel may respect Ms L's demands for nursing care, nutrition, and hydration for her child. Any medical intervention which causes pain, even if it prolongs existence, would be inhumane and contrary to the negative component of the modified principle of respect. Baby L's existence might benefit her mother, but her mother's psychological satisfaction is not sufficient justification for prolonging this child's painful existence. If Baby L's existence is harmful to Baby L, then further treatment is immoral, regardless of the benefits to her mother. A child cannot be treated *solely* as a means to achieve someone else's goals and ends but must be treated simultaneously with respect to her own actual and developing goals and ends.

That another physician was willing to care for this child may be problematic. The report in the *New England Journal of Medicine* is brief and does not explain the other neurologist's reasoning. The decisive question is whether the other neurologist believed that Baby L's life was beneficial to Baby L, or whether the neurologist was promoting her mother's needs. If the former, then Baby L should be transferred to the other neurologist's facility. If the latter, then further treatment is inhumane. When treatment is both virtually futile and inhumane, further treatment is medically and morally impermissible, although third parties may benefit and the treatment may prolong biological existence.[38]

5. Conclusion

Parents are the appropriate decision makers for their children's medical care. The modified principle of respect is a useful guide to examine the limits of parental autonomy. In general, parents ought to provide their children with standard medical care and failure to do so is medically neglectful. State intervention should be limited to (1) cases in which parental refusals are life-threatening or place the child at high risk for serious and significant morbidity *and* the treatment is of proven efficacy with a high likelihood of success; and (2) cases, if they exist, in which parents authorize treatment that is both virtually futile and inhumane.

Notes

1. This need not be their singular focus. The physician may have financial incentives to take care of a particular child, and may offer treatment which serves more to advance profits than to advance the child's well-being. One parent may be using her child as a pawn to save her marriage, or to obtain greater child support from a wealthy but uninvolved father. The child may also have secondary motives for seeking health care, e.g. to avoid school or to focus his parents' attention on him.

2. This example is outdated. Both options were 'standard medical care' in the 1970s and early 1980s, and parents could choose either option. However, by the late 1980s, cranial irradiation was used only in patients who had central nervous system leukaemia or other very high-risk features because of its adverse sequelae, including secondary cancers. See C.-H. Pui, 'Acute Lymphoblastic Leukemia', *Pediatric Clinics of North America*, 44 (August 1997), 831–46. Nevertheless, I use the example because it corresponds to some of the legal cases that helped shape the earlier debate regarding parental refusals of medical care for their children.

3. Studies in the 1970s and 1980s confirmed the inefficacy of laetrile (Amygdalin) and demonstrated its potential for life-threatening toxicity from cyanide poisoning. See, for example, J. H. Price and J. A. Price, 'Laetrile—An Overview', *Journal of School Health*, 48 (1978), 409–16; R. T. Dorr and J. Paxinos, 'The Current Status of Laetrile', *Annals of Internal Medicine*, 89 (1978), 389–97; and C. G. Moertel et al., 'A Clinical Trial of Amygdalin (Laetrile) in the Treatment of Human Cancer', *New England Journal of Medicine*, 306 (1982), 201–6. Despite the data, many patients sought this treatment, particularly when their cancer recurred after a course of chemotherapy. See, for example, J. C. Holland, 'Patients Who Seek Unproven Cancer Remedies: A Psychological Perspective', *Clinical Bulletin*, 11 (1981), 102–5. Similarly, in paediatrics, alternative therapies like laetrile were sought by parents who 'felt desperation . . . [and] were looking for an easier treatment method, and those who were dissatisfied with their role in making treatment decisions' (T. W. Pendergrass and S. Davis, 'Knowledge and Use of Alternative Cancer Therapies in Children', *American Journal of Pediatric Hematology-Oncology*, 3 (1981), 339–445.

4. A 'quick strep' is a rapid diagnostic test to determine if a patient's tonsils carry Group A, beta-hemolytic streptococcus, the organism which causes streptococcal pharyngitis (strep throat).

5. The scenario is not uncommon. Data reveal that many prescriptions written in emergency rooms go unfilled, and that many of those that are filled are taken improperly. In a review of the literature, Shope found that compliance with medication in the paediatric setting ranged from 7 to 89 per cent. The data are summarized by J. T. Shope, 'Medication Compliance', *Pediatric Clinics of North America*, 28 (1981), 7–11. Differences are due to many factors: (1) whether the prescription is for an acute or chronic condition requiring short-term or long-term therapy, respectively; (2) whether the prescription is written by a private physician or by a clinic physician; (3) the frequency of dosing; (4) the demographic features of the patient and his or her family, and so

on. These factors are discussed in detail in Shope, 'Compliance', 12–20. More specifically, compliance with antibiotics average about 75 per cent initially, but less than 25 per cent of patients complete the full course. See B. Stephenson et al., 'Is This Patient Taking the Treatment as Prescribed?', *JAMA*, 269 (1993), 279.

6. The concept of 'medical indications' and 'medically indicated treatment' has been rejected by some ethicists because it is used by physicians as a matter of fact, whereas they argue that it includes subjective values. See, for example, R. M. Veatch, *The Patient-Physician Relation* (Bloomington: Indiana University Press, 1991), Chap. 5: 'The Concept of "Medical Indications"'. I do not deny the uncertainty intrinsic to medical diagnoses and treatments, nor do I deny that what constitutes 'standard medical care' or 'medically indicated' therapy represents probabilistic assessments and entails value judgements regarding risks and benefits. Nevertheless, when the benefit/risk of a particular treatment is sufficiently high, despite the lack of certainty, parents who fail to provide their child with the treatment are judged medically neglectful. The question of when judgements of medical neglect should be enforced is a separate issue which I address in section 3.

7. In the early 1980s, the cure rate for ALL was slightly over 50 per cent. C. H. Kempe, H. K. Silver, and D. O'Brien, *Current Pediatric Diagnosis and Treatment*, 7th ed. (Los Altos, Calif.: Lange Medical Publications, 1982), 896. The cure rate is now closer to two-thirds (Pui, 'Acute Lymphoblastic Leukemia', 831–2).

8. There have been at least two court cases that dealt with this issue: Custody of a minor, 1978 Mass. Adv. Sh. 20002, 379 N.E.2d 1053 (1978), *rev'd and aff'd* 1979 Mass. Adv. Sh. 2124, 393 N.E.2d 386 (1979), and *In re* Hofbauer, 65 A.D.2d 108, 411 N.Y.S.2d 416 (1978), *aff'd* 47 N.Y.2d 1009, 419 N.Y.S.2d 936 (1979). These cases are discussed in section 3.

9. See, for example, *In re* Green, 448 Pa. 338, 292 A.2d 387 (1972), and *In re* Seiferth, 309 N.Y. 80; 127 N.E.2d 820 (1955).

10. State intervention should rarely be sought, particularly when the family is intimate. State intervention in a non-intimate family can be justified at a lower threshold, but even then, state supervision should be limited to those cases in which the state can intervene efficiently and effectively.

11. Note that the parents' decision must be contrary to the child's basic interest. It is not enough to argue that the parents' decision is inconsistent with the child's best interest because parents are only obligated to promote their child's basic interests.

12. Goldstein, Freud, and Solnit propose this term in J. Goldstein, A.

Freud, and A. Solnit, *Before the Best Interests of the Child* (New York: Free Press, 1979), 24–5.

13. Goldstein, Fred, and Solnit, *Before the Best Interests*, 91.

14. *In re* Hofbauer, 419 N.Y.2d 936 (1979).

15. *Custody of a minor*, 393 N.E.2d 836 (1979). Of note is that the court distinguished its finding from the New York ruling in *Hofbauer* on the basis that in this case, there was *no credible medical disagreement*. Given that the Hofbauer's physician was not an oncologist, I believe that there was no *credible* medical disagreement in the *Hofbauer* case, and that Joseph should have received court-ordered chemotherapy.

16. Goldstein, Freud, and Solnit, *Before the Best Interests*, 93–4. The authors define success as the ability 'to have either a life worth living or a life of relatively normal healthy growth' (93–4). I will discuss these two qualifiers with the third criterion.

17. This does not mean that a family or community must spend all of its money to fulfil the basic needs of every member. Consider, again, Amy Smith, the nine-year-old with cerebral palsy. A community need not invest all of its resources to teach Amy to walk independently. At minimum, though, the community ought to help Amy achieve locomotion whether by training her to use crutches or to use a wheelchair. Decisions as to how much money a community should earmark to programs which help members fulfil their basic needs cannot be determined a priori. They will depend, in part, on the technology and resources available within the community. While I believe that communities should give the attainment of activities of daily living a high priority, I do not believe that a community should exhaust all of its resources so that other community programs and services go unfunded.

    It is also the case that not all handicapped individuals can be trained to become physically independent. To be autonomous does not require physical independence. It is more important, then, that handicapped persons be given the services needed to achieve autonomy.

18. W. Sokolosky, 'The Sick Child and the Reluctant Parent—A Framework for Judicial Intervention', *Journal of Family Law*, 20 (1981–2), 77–8.

19. Sokolosky, 'A Framework for Judicial Intervention', 78.

20. Sokolosky, 'A Framework for Judicial Intervention', 87.

21. Sokolosky, 'A Framework for Judicial Intervention', 85–8.

22. Goldstein, Freud, and Solnit do not explore what success rate is high enough to require state intervention. Nor will I, as this number is not necessarily a static concept, but can vary depending on the technology and resources available to the community.

23. Goldstein, Freud, and Solnit, *Before the Best Interests*, 94.
24. Kelsey, 'Shall These Children Live? A Conversation with Dr. Raymond S. Duff', *Reflections*, 72 (1975), 7, as cited in Goldstein, Freud, and Solnit, *Before the Best Interests*, 97.
25. The original Regulations went much further but they were eventually overturned by the courts. Some features, however, were incorporated as amendments into the Child Abuse Statutes. See the Child Abuse Amendments of 1984 42 U.S.C. §§ 5101–05, 5111–13, 5115, (1982 and Supp. 1987), 45 C.F.R. § 1340 (1989).
26. Again, I do not give a number as to what qualifies as a 'high certainty in diagnosis', 'a high likelihood of cure', or 'likely to harm'. These numbers may vary depending on the technology and resources available within the community.
27. K. Faber-Langendoen, 'Resuscitation of Patients with Metastatic Cancer: Is Transient Benefit Still Futile?', *Archives of Internal Medicine*, 151 (1991), 235–9.
28. See, for example, H. Brody, *The Healer's Power* (New Haven, Conn.: Yale University Press, 1992), Chap. 11, 'The Power to Determine Futility', 173–85; Faber-Langendoen, 'Is Transient Benefit Still Futile?', 235–9; J. D. Lantos et al., 'The Illusion of Futility in Clinical Practice', *American Journal of Medicine*, 87 (1989), 81–4; T. Tomlinson and H. Brody, 'Futility and the Ethics of Resuscitation', *JAMA*, 264 (1990), 1276–80; R. Truog, A. Brett, and J. Frader, 'The Problem with Futility', *New England Journal of Medicine*, 326 (1992), 1560–4; and S. Youngner, 'Who Defines Futility?', *JAMA*, 260 (1988), 2094–5.
29. Even this notion of futility is contested. Some ethicists argue that the performance of physiologically futile acts may serve significant symbolic or psychological needs of the patient or her family (Tomlinson and Brody, 'Futility', and Lantos et al., 'The Illusion'). Others argue that the subclassification of physiological futility is really a misnomer for treatment that is physically impossible or physically implausible, whereas futility signifies treatments which are below a certain threshold of probability or utility. See, for example, L. Schneiderman, N. Jecker, and A. Jonsen, 'Medical Futility: Its Meaning and Ethical Implications', *Annals of Internal Medicine*, 112 (1990), 949–54.
30. Nevertheless, a health care provider should not be forced to treat a patient against her own beliefs.
31. Nothing that I have said addresses the issue of (1) who should pay for so-called 'futile' medical treatment; (2) whether insurance companies should offer such coverage; or (3) whether the medical profession as a community can refuse to provide these therapies as 'not medically indicated'.
32. Similarly, one can ask whether there are some treatments where the

treatment entails significant pains, harms, and costs and the likelihood of benefit is so low that physicians should not offer such treatment to patients and their families. This question must be considered with regard to many phase I trials (see Chapter 5.8C), as well as the Baby L case described below.

33. '*Virtually* futile' is the phrase used in many government documents to refer to cases of low-probability, low-efficacy, or poor quality-of-life judgements. It is an acknowledgement that the treatment is not strictly or physiologically futile. 'Inhumane treatment' is treatment in which the pains, harms, and costs are high, and the benefits to the patient are extremely low or improbable.

34. J. J. Paris, R. K. Crone, and F. Reardon, 'Physicians' Refusal of Requested Treatment: The Case of Baby L', *New England Journal of Medicine*, 322 (1990), 1012–13.

35. Paris, Crone, and Reardon, 'The Case of Baby L', 1013.

36. Paris, Crone, and Reardon, 'The Case of Baby L', 1013.

37. Paris, Crone, and Reardon, 'The Case of Baby L', 1013.

38. One must ask whether phase I chemotherapeutic trials also fit the description of 'virtually futile and inhumane'. Such experimental treatments often entail high pains, harms, and costs and have a very low likelihood of direct benefit to the subject. I believe that such an argument can be made which would prohibit parents from authorizing their child's participation in such experimental care. However, there are two differences between Baby L's care and the child who is a subject of a phase I trial. The first difference is that the phase I trial offers indirect benefits to the community at large. I do not believe that this difference can morally justify the treatment, as it would be treating the child solely as a means for the well-being of the community, which is disrespectful of the child as a developing person. The second difference is the difference in quality of life of the two children if the treatment should work. In general, phase I trials are offered to children who are conscious and capable of meaningful relationships. As such, although the likelihood of benefit is very low; the rare success will add quantity and quality of life to the child from the child's own perspective and from the perspective of those with whom she interacts. In contrast, successful treatment for Baby L can add quantity but not quality of life from the infant's perspective (although it may have significant meaning for her mother). This difference is of great moral significance.

The obvious counter-argument is that defining a treatment as 'virtually futile and inhumane' is still value-laden, and that patients or their surrogates, and not physicians, should have the right to make such quality-of-life decisions. The problem with this argument is that it denies the moral agency of the health care providers. It also assumes that just because a medical treatment is possible, it is morally permissible. In contrast, I believe that physicians *qua* professionals must define what are and what are not the appropriate goals of medicine. Such a project would require its own book.

8

The Sexually Active Adolescent

1. *Liberal Respect for Diversity*

There is a contradiction between the purported acceptance of diverse lifestyles within a liberal community and our present-day policy regarding contraceptives for minors. In a liberal community, it is supposed that adults have a special insight into their own conception of the good life, which they can pass on to their children. Yet recent legislation and court decisions in the United States usurp parental power on health care issues pertaining to adolescent sexuality and reproduction.[1]

Consider the following scenario: the Joneses are devout Catholics. Their third daughter, Jane, is fourteen years old. Jane, who has become sexually active with her eighteen-year-old boyfriend Eric, asks her paediatrician for a prescription for oral contraceptives. She knows that her parents disapprove of premarital sexual activity, and that birth control is strictly prohibited by their religion. Genuine respect for different values would require respect for the Joneses' decisions to raise their daughters according to strict Catholic doctrine. They have simplified this by enrolling her in a Catholic parochial school which does not teach the students about human sexuality, birth control, and abortion.

Jane's parents strict prohibition against premarital sexual activity and sex education is not a form of neglect. On the contrary, the Joneses are offering their children a coherent, viable lifestyle—a lifestyle which they believe would be threatened by such education outside the context of marriage. And yet the Joneses cannot fully shelter their daughters because sexuality is pervasive in the mass media and literature. The Joneses recognize this risk, and expend much energy in monitoring their children's exposure to television programmes and movies that address sexuality.

Nevertheless, if Jane is truly bent on obtaining the facts about human sexuality, she can go to the public library!

A liberal community must be tolerant of various lifestyles. As such, our laws allow parents to remove their children from exposure to sex education in the public schools as well as to send their children to private schools in which sexuality is intentionally omitted from the curriculum, or if addressed, is taught as a moral and not a biologic issue. And yet states also have specific statutes (specialized consent statutes) which allow Jane and her paediatrician to discuss contraceptives and allow for Jane to be given a prescription for birth control pills, all without parental consent or parental notification. That the laws are inconsistent in the way that they respect various lifestyles is not surprising; different policies were set by different people with different agendas.

In this chapter, I focus on the question of whether adolescents should be able to procure prescription contraceptives confidentially from their physicians as is presently permitted under the specialized consent statutes. I argue that these statutes fail to give adequate respect to parental autonomy and to the child's need for parental guidance. I argue that the modified principle of respect for persons supports parental involvement.

2. *Exemptions to Parental Consent in Health Care Decision Making*

In a liberal community, parents have the legal right to raise their children according to their own values, and to make major education, religious, and social decisions for them. Within the context of therapeutic health care, parents are presumed to be the child's proxy for minor as well as serious conditions. In general, physicians can neither examine nor treat a child without parental consent. If they do, they can be charged with assault and battery.

There are four exceptions in the United States. First, parental permission is not required but is assumed in an emergency. Some states require an attempt to locate the parents, other relatives, or that the physician consult with at least one other physician. If a parent refuses consent in an emergency, the attending physician can override parental objection without waiting for court permission. This contrasts greatly with adult medical care, in which a competent adult can refuse emergency care even in a life-threatening situation.

Second, parental permission is not mandatory if the minor is emancipated. An emancipated minor is extended all legal capacities as if the minor were of the age of majority. What characterizes a minor as emancipated depends on state law, but includes the following acts of release: marriage, economic independence (especially if the individual is living in separate quarters), parental abandonment, entry into the armed services, and pregnancy.

Nor is parental permission required for mature minors. A mature minor is one who is capable of appreciating the nature and importance of the decision for which he consents. Most states enforce a minimum age, usually between fourteen to sixteen, above which a minor can be deemed mature and allowed to make decisions. Nevertheless, some states limit the type of decisions to which these minors can consent (e.g. uncomplicated and therapeutic health care which entails low risk).

Third, the state does not require parental permission if it has a substantial compelling interest such as universal vaccinations (which it can require of *all* its citizens, both children and adults).[2]

Fourth, all fifty states have specialized consent statutes, statutes which vary in their scope, but which give adolescents some autonomy to seek and consent independently to drug and alcohol abuse treatment, treatment for sexually transmitted diseases, and contraceptive counselling.[3] Some states even allow minors to consent to abortions without disclosure or consent from their parents.[4] The statutes were designed to encourage adolescents to seek health care for problems which they might deny, ignore, or delay if they had to get parental permission.

From a public health perspective, the purpose of the specialized consent statutes is laudable; namely, to encourage early, responsible sexual health care for adolescents. But the empirical data do not support the claim that adolescents will seek medical care for sexual and reproductive issues even if they are assured complete confidentiality. Despite the passage of the specialized consent statutes in the 1960s, rates of adolescent pregnancy and sexually transmitted diseases continue to increase.[5] The data also show that most adolescents (especially those younger than sixteen) discuss these issues with their parents.[6] Can the specialized consent statutes be morally justified?

3. *The Arguments in Favour of the Specialized Consent Statutes and Why They Fail*

Those who support the specialized consent statutes offer several pragmatic and moral justifications. The pragmatic position is compelling: given that they are frequently sexually active even when birth control and other sexual health services are relatively inaccessible, adolescents need to be given the opportunity to be responsible for their sexual activity. The pragmatist does not need to concede or refute whether the availability of such services increases the number of sexually active adolescents because the number is sufficiently large, even when services are unavailable, that it portends a public health crisis.

The problem with the pragmatist's position is that it depends upon two assumptions: one, that adolescents are competent to make these decisions, and two, that a policy that grants adolescents autonomy will achieve greater sexual responsibility than would a policy that requires parental involvement. Consider if the two assumption are false. If the first assumption is false, that is, if adolescents are not competent to make health care decisions, then the statutes are misdirected. If adolescents are incapable of giving informed consent in the area of sexual and reproductive health services, then the statutes unfairly hold them responsible for such measures. If the second assumption is false, that is, if granting autonomy to adolescents does not produce greater sexual responsibility, then the argument for extending autonomy fails. Because parents have presumptive responsibility for their minor children, even if they are competent, legislation should override their responsibility only if it can be shown that the policies will promote adolescent well-being *significantly better* than a policy based on parental responsibility; otherwise, the state should defer to parental authority.

Is the first assumption valid? Are adolescents competent to make health care decisions? Although the data support the claim that adolescents and adults make equally competent decisions in medical vignettes designed by psychologists,[7] this competency may not apply to real life. Despite their knowledge regarding automobile safety, adolescents account for a disproportionate number of fatal car accidents. And despite their ability to repeat the facts about the transmission of AIDS and other sexually transmitted diseases, adolescents tend to overlook long-term consequences. If competency is understood as the ability both *to choose and to act* to promote one's self-interest, then the claim that adolescents are competent is not persuasive.

The second assumption, that the specialized consent statutes will promote significantly better health care for adolescents in the realm of sexual and reproductive services than if adolescents were required to get parental involvement, is also unpersuasive. Despite the confidentiality assured by the specialized consent statutes, adolescents typically delay seeking sexual and reproductive health care for almost one year after they become sexually active.[8] If parental involvement causes adolescents to delay such services indefinitely, then the statutes achieve significantly better results. Proponents of these statutes need to obtain empirical data that show that adolescents will seek earlier and better care if they are assured complete confidentiality. Because such data do not exist, the presumption ought to be in favour of parental involvement.

The proposed legislation must produce *significantly better* results because of the presumptive moral authority of parents. The state should not override parental autonomy and give adolescents sole decision-making authority on a single issue because such state intervention may inadvertently undermine parental autonomy in other realms, realms in which we both need and want enduring parental commitment. The state should be wary of intervening, *unless* the state is able and willing (which it is not) to take responsibility for all of the other concerns of its adolescent citizens. Thus, unless granting adolescent autonomy will promote significantly better sexual and reproductive health care for adolescents, the state should not create policies that override parental autonomy.

A second pragmatic argument in favour of adolescent autonomy in sexual and reproductive health care is based on the concern of domestic violence. Some adolescents may seek sexual and reproductive health care without parental knowledge because these adolescents fear potential parental abuse. They believe that their parents would be so outraged that they would harm them. It is notable that many adolescents who make such claims have never been abused and there are no data to support their fears.[9] Scant data show that parents react much less negatively than adolescents anticipate, even when parental involvement is mandated.[10] If the adolescents' fears are invalid, the statutes deny parental autonomy to the vast majority of parents who are both able and willing to guide their adolescent's reproductive and sexual medical care and who consider this role integral to their childrearing rights and responsibilities.

Even if there are some adolescents whose fears are valid, the statutes are still too intrusive a method to protect them. Rather, in those cases in which parents become abusive when confronted by their child's sexuality, child abuse statutes and child and youth service programs are in place to protect the adolescents and to ensure that they get appropriate medical care.

A third pragmatic argument to support adolescent autonomy is that confidentiality avoids conflict. Some adolescents want to act without parental consent because they know that their parents' religious convictions condemn premarital sexual activity and birth control. Although parents can remove their children from sex education classes because we supposedly respect their traditional lifestyle, physicians can go behind their backs and prescribe birth control to their daughters.[11] Would anyone suggest that we should not tell parents when their adolescents are failing in school to avoid conflict? Poor grades are common and are a major cause of intrafamilial strife. All three pragmatic arguments are weak at best.

The moral argument supporting the specialized consent statutes is based on the claim that competency should entail autonomy. This argument depends upon two assumptions that I rejected in Chapter 4: one, that the competency of children is not morally different from the competency of adults, so that competent children and competent adults should be treated similarly, and two, that competency is necessary and sufficient to justify autonomy. To argue that competency should entail autonomy ignores the fact that parents are responsible for responding to the child's current identity, needs, and interests *and* for shaping the child's future identity, needs, and interests. Parents are responsible for steering their child's developing personhood, a duty which is usurped if children are granted sole decision-making autonomy regarding their basic medical needs. Parents may choose to restrict their child's present-day autonomy to enhance or guide his or her overall or long-term autonomy.

Parents also have a valid third-party interest in the child's development and activities, even after she has achieved a significant level of competency. In general, parental decision-making autonomy serves both the children and the parents. It serves the children to have autonomous parents who will help them become autonomous individuals. It serves the adults' interest in having and raising a family according to their own vision of the good life. This freedom does not automatically stop when the child becomes competent. If anything, parents now have the opportunity to try to inculcate their beliefs through rational discourse, instead of through example, bribery, or force. While children are still dependent upon their parents for emotional, economic, and material support, parental interest in making decisions for their children must be balanced against the competent children's interest in acting autonomously. In contrast, the present-day specialized consent statutes give unilateral responsibility to adolescents who can still benefit from adult guidance, and deny enduring parental interest in educating and guiding their competent children according to their own values.

The specialized consent statutes are also illiberal in that they support those particular conceptions of the good life which accept or at least condone responsible adolescent sexual activity. These statutes allow sexually active adolescents to circumvent parents who forbid premarital sexual activity. A liberal community should accommodate families that hold a wide spectrum of attitudes towards sexuality, and respect that these families may seek to structure the experience of their children according to these values. As such, a truly liberal community might allow the Joneses to prevent Jane from procuring all contraceptives and from aborting a foetus, if conceived. A truly liberal community must tolerate non-liberal but legitimate (i.e. non-abusive, non-neglectful) lifestyles. Specialized consent statutes circumvent parental decision-making autonomy inappropriately. And they do so, in some cases, without parental awareness that they are being excluded.

4. *Arguments in Favour of Rescinding the Specialized Consent Statutes*

There are several reasons why we ought to rescind the specialized consent statutes. First, they send adolescents the wrong message. They teach adolescents that their decisions regarding sexuality are unrelated to other aspects of their lives. Consider that parents dictate what schools and church their children attend and in which activities their children may participate, but these same children have legal sanction to ignore parental autonomy in the area of sexuality. Consider that these children cannot consent to a throat culture without parental permission,[12] but can authorize their physicians to perform a pelvic examination.

Second, the specialized consent statutes affirm the adolescents' attitude that sexuality is solely a private matter. It is not. Adolescent sexual activity has numerous public consequences for which the adolescent is ill prepared to accept responsibility: responsibility to themselves, by delaying sexual gratification until they are emotionally and psychologically prepared; responsibility to their partners, by practicing safe sex; and responsibility to their community, by avoiding parenthood until they are both emotionally and financially capable of caring for a child.

Third, parents are presumed to be the decision makers for their children because parents are best situated to decide and to act upon what is in their children's best interest, and because parents are financially and socially responsible for them. This ought to be no less true of medical care with regard to sexual health issues.

By arguing against the specialized consent statutes, I do not deny the need for a public commitment to prevent and treat the unwanted consequences of adolescent sexual activity. In that regard, the specialized consent statutes are on the mark; they affirm the belief that the cost of unwanted adolescent pregnancy and untreated sexually transmitted diseases is too high. But the implementation of these statutes entails moral hurdles for the ethical physician, including collusion with adolescents against their parents,[13] disrespect for parental conceptions of the good, and a disregard for the adolescent's need for further parental guidance.

Parents have both a right and a responsibility to make health care decisions for (or at least with) their children. Parental autonomy should be presumed and defeased only if the parents'

decisions do not respect the child's developing and partially actualized personhood. Generally, parental involvement in their
child's sexual and reproductive health care is consistent with the
modified principle of respect. Parents are responsible for promoting their child's present and future interests and identity. Parents
play a leading role in their child's sexual identity, their sexual attitudes and mores, and the manner in which they give their sexuality expression. Parents must realize that it is their responsibility
and prerogative to teach their child their own values, including
their values on sexuality. During their child's earliest years, parents are the child's sole source of sex education. As the child
matures, parents ought to discuss issues of human sexuality, intimacy, and reproduction with their children because to omit this
will impede the child's ability to make autonomous choices in this
important aspect of personal identity and fulfilment (positive
component of the modified principle of respect). By playing a
central role in Jane's sexual and reproductive health care decisions, Jane's parents can try to influence her behaviour and guide
her into the adult that they want her to become. Even if Jane
opposes their beliefs, her parents have both the right and the
responsibility to try to steer her sexual expression in a way consistent with their beliefs. As an adult, if Jane continues to believe
that her parents' decision did not respect her evolving sexuality,
their actions have not prevented her from premarital sexual
expression at a later date. At minimum, their restrictions may
have prevented her from untoward sexually transmitted diseases,
which could have had adverse consequences for her adult sexual
expression and procreative abilities.

Parental involvement in reproductive and sexual health care is
also not abusive or neglectful (negative component of the modified principle of respect), unless an adolescent's parents become
abusive when their involvement is requested. Rather, parents are
neglectful if they ignore this responsibility. Parents are responsible for their child's moral and physical development of which
sexuality and procreative attitudes are integral components.
Statutes which encourage adolescents to circumvent their parents' awareness of their sexual activity place adolescents at risk
for making sexual and reproductive health care decisions that will
not be in their long-term interest. They also place adolescents at
risk for sexual exploitation from older, more sophisticated sexual

partners.[14] Parental involvement in these decisions may prevent abuse and exploitation. Thus, parental involvement and authority in sexual and reproductive health care decisions are consistent with both components of the modified principle of respect for persons.

A serious objection to rescinding the specialized consent statutes and requiring parental authorization for prescription-requiring contraceptives is that it is unrealistic and will result in more adolescent pregnancies. Presently, approximately one million adolescents become pregnant yearly, and most of these adolescents are unmarried and their pregnancies are unplanned. There are inadequate data to prove or disprove that parental involvement will lead to more or fewer pregnancies.[15] Rather, as Michael Lynskey notes, '[T]he specialized consent statutes were introduced largely on the basis of the *a priori* belief that they would . . . reduce risks of unwanted pregnancy and sexually transmitted diseases.'[16] The issue, then, is what we should do in the absence of such evidence. Lynskey argues for the status quo. I believe that without such evidence we should respect parental autonomy, as we do in all other health care settings.[17]

Another objection to rescinding the specialized consent statutes is the greater negative impact it would have on adolescent females versus adolescent males. According to this objection, the specialized consent statutes are a part of the whole package that ensures *all* women the right to procreative freedom and control over their own bodies. To rescind the specialized consent statutes would be to diminish women's autonomy in the sexual and reproductive arenas.

This argument fails because it is overinclusive. Adult women *must* have full control over their own bodies, including public support for family planning clinics, pregnancy-related services including abortion services and prenatal care, rape-counselling programs, and public clinics where sexually transmitted diseases are treated and patients are counselled regarding HIV. But we can and must distinguish adult women and female adolescents. Adolescents who live at home with their families must involve their families in their health care.[18]

I mean no harm to either female or male adolescents by supporting rescission of the specialized consent statutes. In general, females need more sexual and reproductive health care than males, but that reality involves responsibility as well as privilege, for only females have the capacity to conceive and bear a child. That this biologic fact gives female adolescents less sexual freedom as adolescents (and as adults, at least in our contemporary culture), is surely outweighed by the fact that these same individuals have greater reproductive opportunities as adults.[19]

5. *Over-the-Counter Contraceptives*

Unfortunately, there are adolescents who are sexually active and are unwilling to discuss their decision with their parents. If the specialized consent statutes are rescinded, these adolescents will have no access to sexual and reproductive health care. Given my arguments in support of parental involvement, it may seem that I should accept this consequence. I would if the consequences of adolescent sexuality, namely adolescent pregnancy and adolescent parenthood, were private events. They are not. There are emotional, physical, and financial obligations of parenthood that most adolescents cannot fulfil. And even more worrisome is the impact on their children. Children of adolescent parents often have more behaviour problems and are at greater risk for significant morbidity and mortality from accidents than children born to adult women. In the long term, children of adolescent parents are more likely to be high-school drop-outs, adolescent delinquents, as well as adolescent parents themselves.[20] As such, adolescent pregnancy is a public health crisis.

One approach to the public health crisis is to require parental involvement in the procurement of prescription contraceptives but to keep over-the-counter birth control easily accessible to all individuals, even minors.[21] The justification for this solution is pragmatic; a policy which makes over-the-counter birth control easily accessible to all individuals, even minors, is neither an attempt to override parental moral values nor a statement condoning adolescent sexual activity. Rather the justification to have barrier method birth control available to all adolescents is consequentialistic: the cost of denial is unwanted adolescent pregnancy and diseases, which are a larger community burden than we are willing to accept. The solution also has a deontological basis: the adolescent's procurement of over-the-counter contraceptives does not involve deception nor undermining of parental authority by medical providers.

Many of the moral arguments I use to argue against prescribing birth control confidentially to adolescents could be used to require parental permission for the purchase of over-the-counter contraceptives.[22] Richard Fern argues that a truly liberal community could restrict access to over-the-counter contraceptives as well as prescription-requiring contraceptives.[23] Depending on where a particular liberal society defines the balance between family autonomy and public health, he may be right. There is, however, a significant moral difference: the need for a physician's prescription. The purchase of over-the-counter contraceptives does not involve deception by a health care provider and does not place the physician in the situation where his or her actions undermine parental values and authority. As such, over-the-counter contraceptives are consistent with respect for parental autonomy, where the specialized consent statutes are not.

6. *Adolescents' Right to Privacy*

An alternate argument against parental involvement in their children's reproductive and sexual decisions is based on the right to privacy. Legally, the right to privacy is not explicitly found in the Constitution or its Amendments, but various Supreme Court rulings have located this right within the penumbra of the Constitution.[24] To a lesser extent, children have a right to privacy, although it can be abridged more easily than that of their adult counterpart.[25]

To argue for confidential sexual and reproductive health care for adolescents on the grounds of a right to privacy, one must argue that the right to privacy trumps the right of parents to raise their children according to their own conception of the good.[26] The question of how the courts ought to balance the parents' right to raise a family against a child's right to privacy has been addressed only twice by a federal district court. In both cases, the court upheld the balance in favour of the parents' rights.[27] The court did not deny that adolescents have a constitutional right to privacy. Rather, the court argued that the child's right to privacy can be outweighed by parental and family autonomy.

Adolescents have a need and a moral right to privacy. In particular, adolescents need some freedom to adjust to their emerging sexuality, to adapt to their changing bodies, and to understand their emotional needs. A parent who insists on reading a child's diary, or who does not allow an adolescent to have privacy during her annual physical, is disrespectful. But a child's need for sexual privacy does not require reproductive and sexual health care decision-making autonomy. Parents should retain decision-making autonomy, provided that their decisions respect the child's developing and partially actualized personhood.

7. Conclusion

The specialized consent statutes were designed to empower adolescents with decision-making autonomy with respect to their sexuality. But to do this, the statutes permitted or even encouraged adolescents to circumvent their parents and the guidance they might offer. The statutes are inconsistent with the respect owed to parents within a liberal community. I favour laws that allow parents to decide upon the nature of their children's sex education and laws which require parental involvement in the procurement of medical care pertaining to adolescent sexual activity. I also favour laws which allow sexually active adolescents who refuse to involve their parents to have access to over-the-counter barrier methods of birth control. This enables these adolescents to avoid the unwanted consequences of their decision without legitimizing disrespect for parental autonomy by other institutions. It is a liberal community's way of avoiding a lose-lose solution in a no-win situation.

Notes

1. In Great Britain, the *Gillick* decision parallels this move. The case addressed whether adolescents should be able to consent to contraceptive treatment. The House of Lords rejected an age-based standard and concluded that any child can give consent provided that he or she has 'sufficient understanding and intelligence to enable to understand fully what is proposed' (Gillick v. W Norfolk & Wisbech

HA [1985] 3 All ER 402, 421). Although child liberationists lament several post-*Gillick* cases which limit this ruling (see, for example, *Re* R [1991] 4 All ER 177; *Re* W [1992] 4 All ER 627; and *Re* E [1993] 1 FLR 386), none of these cases addressed contraceptives or other sexuality-related health care issues. The post-*Gillick* cases give parents the right to consent for a treatment that a child refuses, but none of these cases suggests that a parent can prohibit medical care to which the child consents.

2. Jacobson v. Massachusetts, 197 U.S. 11 (1905).

3. A. R. Holder, *Legal Issues in Pediatrics and Adolescent Medicine*, 2nd ed. (New Haven, Conn.: Yale University Press, 1985).

4. This chapter does not address the issue of abortion, nor should the reader extrapolate my position on the role of parental consent and/or notification from my arguments regarding oral contraceptives and the treatment of sexually transmitted diseases. Although I do not believe that a foetus is a moral person, the foetus does add further complexities to the public and private dimensions of adolescent sexual activity which require a separate analysis.

5. Anonymous, 'Sexual Behavior Among High School Students—United States, 1990', *MMWR—Morbidity and Mortality Weekly Report*, 40 (1992), 885–8. See also A. M. Spitz et al., 'Pregnancy, Abortion and Birth Rates Among U.S. Adolescents—1980, 1985, and 1990', *JAMA*, 275 (1996), 989–94. To be accurate, pregnancy rates increased by approximately 8 per cent between 1980 and 1990, although the pregnancy rate among sexually active teenagers decreased. The difference is due to the increasing number of sexually active adolescents.

6. These data were culled from a variety of studies which were summarized and discussed by the Council on Scientific Affairs of the American Medical Association, 'Council Report: Confidential Health Services for Adolescents', *JAMA*, 269 (1993), 1422. Of note, the Council's emphasis was to show that the other adolescents stated that they would avoid medical care if parental notification were required, but as the authors of a corollary article in the same issue of *JAMA* note, '[W]hat adolescents say they will do (i.e, regarding forgoing care) may be different from what they actually do.' T. Cheng et al., 'Confidentiality in Health Care: A Survey of Knowledge, Perceptions and Attitudes Among High School Students', *JAMA*, 269 (1993), 1406.

7. Many of the data are summarized in two review articles: T. Grisso and L. Vierling, 'Minors' Consent to Treatment: A Developmental Perspective', *Professional Psychology*, 9 (1978), 412–27; and L. Weithorn and S. Campbell, 'The Competency of Children and Adolescents to Make Informed Treatment Decisions', *Child Development*, 53 (1982), 1589–98.

8. American Academy of Pediatrics, Committee on Adolescence, 'Contraception and Adolescents', *Pediatrics*, 86 (1990), 134, citing L. S. Zabin and S. D. Clark, 'Why They Delay: A Study of Teenage Family Planning Clinic Patients', *Family Planning Perspectives*, 13 (1981), 205–17.

9. Except for the high rate of adolescent abuse in general. See, Council on Scientific Affairs of the American Medical Association, 'Adolescents as Victims of Family Violence', *JAMA*, 270 (1993), 1850–6. But there are no data to show that parental notification contributes to this abuse.

10. See the various studies cited by E. L. Worthington et al., 'Mandatory Parental Involvement Prior to Adolescent Abortion', *Journal of Adolescent Health*, 12 (1991), 139.

11. Morally, I believe that parents should be allowed to remove their children from sex education courses which go against their moral beliefs because it is the responsibility and prerogative of parents to teach their child their own values, including their values on sexuality. Parents play a leading role in their child's sexual identity, their sexual attitudes and mores, and the manner in which they give their sexuality expression. Pragmatically, I would also add, sex education has not worked. Sex education has not been shown to change risky behaviour. See, for example, B. A. Cromer and R. T. Brown, 'Update on Pregnancy, Condom Use, and Prevalence of Selected Sexually Transmitted Diseases in Adolescents', *Current Opinion in Obstetrics and Gynecology*, 4 (1992), 855–9; U.S. Congress, Office of Technology Assessment, *Adolescent Health, i: Background and the Effectiveness of Selected Prevention and Treatment Services* (Washington, DC: U.S. Government Printing Office, 1992), 365; M. Durbin et al., 'Factors Associated with Multiple Sex Partners Among Junior High School Students', *Journal of Adolescent Health*, 14 (1993), 202–7; L. C. Ku, F. C. Sonenstein, and J. H. Pleck, 'The Association of AIDS Education and Sex Education with Sexual Behavior and Condom Use Among Teenage Men', *Family Planning Perspectives*, 24 (1992), 100–6; H. H. Cagampang, R. P. Barth, M. Korpi, and D. Kirby, 'Education Now and Babies Later (ENABL): Life History of a Campaign to Postpone Sexual Involvement', *Family Planning Perspectives*, 19 (1997), 109–14.

Nevertheless, one could take the position that all knowledge is good. On that basis, one can argue that sex education should be incorporated into school curricula and that parents should not be allowed to remove their children from such teaching. If we as a society agree that explicit sex education is necessary, then this is a political decision which I can accept. But I would also be tolerant if Jane's parochial school taught these facts infused with value-laden moral judgements.

To refuse such value-laden instruction is to insist upon one conception of the human good which the liberal state *qua* liberal state cannot do.

12. I realize that this is also changing under the mature minor statutes which allow 'mature' adolescents to consent to much of their own medical care. G. S. Sigman and C. O'Connor, 'Exploration for Physicians of the Mature Minor Doctrine', *Journal of Pediatrics*, 119 (1991), 520–5. Nevertheless, this freedom is not commonly sought when the issue is not sexual, reproductive, or psychiatric. Rather, in general, parents are an important influence in their children's decisions and adolescents tend to seek their support and advice in most other matters. See L. B. Hendry, W. Roberts, A. Glendinning, and J. C. Coleman, 'Adolescents' Perception of Significant Individuals in Their Lives', *Journal of Adolescence*, 15 (1992), 255–70. In addition, adolescents are often willing to conform to parental influence (see D. G. Scherer and N. D. Reppucci, 'Adolescents' Capacities to Provide Voluntary Informed Consent: The Effects of Parental Influence and Medical Dilemmas', *Law and Human Behavior*, 12 (1988), 123–41), particularly female adolescents (C. Gilligan, N. P. Lyons, and T. J. Hanmer (eds.), *Making Connections: The Relational Worlds of Adolescent Girls at Emma Willard School* (Cambridge, Mass.: Harvard University Press, 1990)).

13. Technically, the statutes do not require physicians to deceive parents, because physicians are under no legal obligation to provide a specific service or treatment requested by a minor if it conflicts with their moral principles. Council on Long Range Planning and Development, *AMA Policy Compendium* (Chicago, Ill.: American Medical Association, 1990), 1. Nevertheless, the point still stands that if the physician confidentially gives Jane the prescription that she requests, then the physician effectively has colluded with Jane in deceiving her parents.

14. In two out of three births to teenage mothers, studies indicate the father is twenty years old or older, often much older than the mother. M. Navarro, 'Teen-Age Mothers Viewed as Abused Prey of Older Men', *New York Times*, 19 May 1996, 1 and 11. As Navarro points out, the real magnitude of the problem is not completely known because it is not known 'how many older men are sexual partners of teenage girls who do not have babies' (Navarro, 'Teen-Age Mothers', 11).

15. There are some data to refute the claim. For example, Weed and Olsen's analysis of 1978 birth and pregnancy rates showed 'that rather than the family planners' prediction of 200 to 300 fewer pregnancies for every 1,000 teenagers involved in family planning programs, there was an increase of about 120 pregnancies for every 1,000 teenage family-planning clients'. S. Weed and J. Olsen, 'Effect of

Family-Planning Programs for Teenagers on Adolescent Birth and Pregnancy Rates', *Family Perspectives*, 20 (1986), 160–1, as cited by L. Wardle, 'Parents' Rights vs. Minors' Rights Regarding the Provision of Contraceptives to Teenagers', *Nebraska Law Review*, 68 (1989), 255, n. 218.

In another article, Weed and Olsen review data from other time periods which confirmed 'the strong statistical associations between provisions of family planning services to teenagers and increases in teen pregnancy and abortion rates'. S. Weed and J. Olsen, 'Effects of Family-Planning Programs on Teenage Pregnancy—Replication and Extension', *Family Perspectives*, 20 (1986), 184 and 190, as cited by Wardle, 'Parents Rights vs. Minors' Rights', 255, note 218. If the availability of contraceptives encourages the incidence of sexual activity, then part of the increase can be explained by the fact that adolescents are poor contraceptive users. See data cited by S. J. H. Emans and D. P. Goldstein, *Pediatric and Adolescent Gynecology*, 3rd ed. (Boston, Mass.: Little, Brown, 1990), 456, table 15-2.

16. M. Lynskey, 'Universal Solutions or Individual Choices', *Politics and the Life Sciences*, 15 (1996), 295.

17. A more scientific approach was suggested by Merrill, who proposed that we allow each state to set its own policies and that we gather data prospectively on the impact of confidentiality on teenage sexual activity, pregnancy, and sexually transmitted diseases (R. E. Merrill, personal communication, 1994).

18. The independent minor will still be covered by the emancipated minor statutes in many states.

19. Consider, for example, that the single or lesbian woman can procreate by artificial insemination, whereas paid surrogate mothers for single or gay men are often illegal. At the other end of the spectrum, the pregnant woman has the final right to decide whether to take a pregnancy to term. If abortion were illegal, this part of my argument would be weaker.

20. L. Juszczak, 'Adolescent Parenthood', in S. B. Friedman, M. Fisher, and S. K. Schonberg (eds.), *Comprehensive Adolescent Health Care* (St Louis, Mo.: Quality Medical Publishing, 1992), 1041–6; A. Conseur, F. P. Rivara, R. Barnoski, and I. Emanuel, 'Maternal and Perinatal Risk Factors for Later Delinquency', *Pediatrics*, 99 (1997), 785–90.

21. And in fact, in 1977, the Supreme Court held in Carey v. Population Service International, 431 U.S. 678 (1977), that state laws restricting the availability of over-the-counter contraceptives to minors were unconstitutional. I explain below why I concur with the Court's decision.

22. P. R. Wolpe, 'Adolescent Contraception and the Just Society', *Politics and Life Sciences*, 15 (1996), 321–3.
23. R. L. Fern, 'Adolescent Sexuality and the L-Word: How Liberal a Liberalism', *Politics and the Life Sciences*, 15 (September 1996), 291.
24. Griswold v. Connecticut, 381 U.S. 479, 85 S. Ct. 1678, 14 L. Ed.2d 510 (1965). The right to privacy for adults was further clarified in Roe v. Wade, 410 U.S. 113 (1973).
25. See, for example, Planned Parenthood of Central Missouri v. Danforth, 428 U.S. 52 (1976), and Bellotti v. Baird, 332 U.S. 622 (1979).
26. The right of parents to raise their children according to their own conception of the good is also grounded in the constitution. The landmark case is Meyer v. Nebraska, 262 U.S. 390 (1923). In *Meyer*, the Supreme Court found unconstitutional a law that prohibited parents from sending their children to a school in which German was taught in the first eight grades. The court stated that the Fourteenth Amendment's liberty clause included 'not merely freedom from bodily restraint but also the right of the individual to contract, to engage in any of the common occupations of life, to acquire useful knowledge, to marry, establish a home, and bring up children' (id. at 399). The Court reaffirmed this position in other cases, including two other important education cases. See Pierce v. Society of Sisters, 268 U.S. 510 (1925), and Wisconsin v. Yoder, 406 U.S. 205 (1972).
27. In *Doe v. Irwin*, a federal district court in Michigan heard a case which sought to balance the privacy rights of minors with their parents' right to raise a family. The court found that the failure of state family planning agencies to notify parents violated their fundamental right to raise a family according to their own conception of the good which outweighed the adolescents' competing claims. See Doe v. Irwin, 428 F. Supp. 1198 (W.D. Mich. 1977). After the Supreme Court decided *Carey*, the United States Court of Appeals for the Sixth Circuit vacated and remanded *Irwin*. The federal district court reaffirmed its order and opinion. See Doe v. Irwin, 441 F. Supp. 1247 (W.D. Mich. 1977), *rev'd* 615 F.2d 1162 (6th Cir. 1980), *cert. denied*, 449 U.S. 829 (1980).

9

Conclusion

1. Interpreting What Constrained Parental Autonomy Permits and Requires

In the last four chapters, I have applied the model of constrained parental autonomy to various health care activities. Implementation of this model requires significant changes in what informed consent allows and requires for paediatric health care decisions. The model runs counter to the current trend to increase the health care autonomy of adolescents.[1] For example, parents would be allowed to override their incompetent and competent child's dissent to participate in minimal-risk non-therapeutic research, which parents may not do under the current Federal Regulations. Implementation would also alter the types of health care activities in which children can participate. For example, presently *all* children are potential kidney donors for other family members. I argued that kidney donations from incompetent siblings should be prohibited.

The specific changes that my model would require have two common threads: (1) to return the locus of paediatric health care decision making to the intimate family; and (2) to restrict children's participation in health care activities that fail to protect their developing personhood. The reforms will have political opposition from two distinct groups. My first objective will be opposed by those who argue that the intimate family is a rare entity. These opponents may be conflating 'intimate' with 'ideal'. Despite the changes in the institution of the family, it has functioned throughout all of mankind's history as the primary child-rearing institution. While often not ideal, and frequently less intimate than modern families, it has been successful in its primary function. Policies need to encourage and strengthen the family and promote an environment in which it can flourish.

This requires respect for family privacy and family autonomy, policies supported by the model of constrained parental autonomy.

My second objective will be rejected by those who argue that children are made more vulnerable by social attempts to protect them. Child liberationists maintain that children need equal rights, which I have argued fails to account for the child's need for a protected period in which to develop the skills necessary to flourish and for the parents' right to rear their children according to their *own* conceptions of the good.

I begin with the presumption that the family is a viable institution and a valuable institution for expressions of love and intimacy. I also presume that parents choose to bear, or at least choose to rear their children, and that many of them consider this an integral part of their life plans. These presumptions can be and have been questioned. And yet, with rare exception, philosophers accept the institution of the family and only question its structure and social role.[2] Given these presumptions, I propose a decision-making model for children that locates decision making within the family. The model of constrained parental autonomy also provides a mechanism for conflict resolution. Although parents ought to involve their child in the decision-making process, constrained parental autonomy generally empowers parents to be the final decision makers without public scrutiny or review.

But this does not mean that parental autonomy is without limits. Under my model, parental autonomy is constrained by both the state and the child. The state sets the boundaries within which family decisions are respected and when the child's decision must be respected. Even when the child's decision is not binding, the child's opinion is not irrelevant; children have great influence on their parents, and their opinions should be heard.[3]

2. *Objections to Constrained Parental Autonomy*

I want to consider two potential objections to the model of constrained parental autonomy. First, critics can argue that my model is not demanding enough; either parents should be held to a higher standard or children should demand more of their parents. Second, they can argue that my model empowers parents too much or that my model does not empower children enough. Let me consider each of these objections in turn.

First, it is true that parents ought to go beyond the bare minimum that this model requires. A parent who continuously asks herself whether she has fulfilled all of her duties has asked one question too many.[4] In general, parents are motivated to promote their child's interests; and some will even sacrifice their own interests to give their child every opportunity possible. This may be laudatory, but surely it is not obligatory.

My model is not meant to offer a standard to which parents should strive. In a liberal society, there is no agreement as to what would be the ideal parent or the ideal parent–child relationship. Instead, my model offers a threshold below which parents must not fall. If parents cannot procure (or provide for the procurement of) *all* of their child's basic needs, then the state, as *parens patriae*, must intervene. Although parents are given primary responsibility to fulfil their children's needs, the larger community shares these obligations, as children are members of families and the larger community.

Even if all that we can demand of parents is that they fulfil this minimum threshold, should advocates for children demand more? For example, should we advocate for the promotion of a child's self-regarding best interest claim, as proposed by Allen Buchanan and Dan Brock,[5] even if we must accept that in the real world the child's interests will be balanced against other factors, including the needs and interests of other family members? Such advocacy is not realistic, given that there is no consensus on what the child's best interest is outside of the child's existence in the real world. Rather, a child's best interest is shaped and defined by his parents, although other communities to which the child belongs also play a role. Furthermore, in the real world, the child's interests are intertwined with the interests of his family, making a purely self-regarding best interest claim less useful and less desirable.

The next line of objection refers to the relative empowerment of parents over children. Critics may object that I give too much weight to the parents' values and beliefs and permit parents to place disproportionate weight on their own interests. This is a misunderstanding. Parents have primary responsibility to ensure that *all* of their child's basic needs are met. Parents who weigh their own interests as more significant than their child's basic needs are either malicious or misguided. In either case, their decision is not within the wide autonomy permitted within an intimate family. State intervention may be justified if the state can act efficiently with a high likelihood of success. But if the parents have provided for their child's basic needs, then they can and should have the freedom to balance the child's needs and interests with their own needs, interests, and goals.

A related issue is whether my model disempowers children, particularly competent children. Critics may accept my model as a useful guide for parental decisions regarding their young child, but argue that the model does not give enough respect to the competent child. I do not agree. Parents do themselves and their child a large disfavour by not involving their child in the decision-making process. But this is not the issue; the issue is who should have ultimate authority when there is intrafamilial disagreement. Under my model, the child's dissent should be binding in fewer cases than it presently is. Parental authority to override the child's present-day autonomy is not meant to disempower the child but rather to give him greater lifetime autonomy. I am unwilling to abandon children to their present-day autonomy, given that their decisions are based on limited knowledge and experience. Rather, children need a protected period in which they can develop the virtues and skills necessary for making decisions that will successfully promote their own goals, values, and lifetime autonomy.

3. *Future Issues to Be Explored*

This book is only a start. There are many issues which I leave unexplored and unexamined. First, there is a need for a meta-ethical defence of why respect for persons is the appropriate guidance principle for parent–child relationships. Kant argued that respect for persons was a categorical imperative that applied universally.[6] More recently, Robin Downie and Elizabeth Telfer have shown how respect can apply in both the personal and impersonal settings.[7] But how and why respect should govern intrafamilial relationships needs further philosophical explication.

Second, constrained parental autonomy is a model about decision making for children in intimate families, but it is not an algorithm. The positive and negative components of the modified principle of respect offer some guidance regarding the standards a child's surrogate should use, but what each component requires may differ in different health care settings. It also depends on the concepts of relative risks and relative benefits about which there is no consensus in the medical community, let alone in the general community. Nowhere do I offer principled criteria that would explain why I chose to draw the lines where I did. In part, my interpretation is based on my empirical understanding of the degrees and probabilities of risks and benefits that the activity produces for the child and her family. It would be useful to have a principled strategy that would allow readers to draw guidelines for every possible health care situation.

Third, the presumption that families are intimate until proven otherwise leaves some children vulnerable, which raises the need for a full explication of the characteristics and qualities that define an intimate parent–child relationship.

Fourth, constrained parental autonomy applies only to decisions made within an intimate family context. It may be possible to modify the principle of respect further to account for non-intimate families. If not, other principles should be adopted.

Children are a vulnerable population because of their dependency. The medical ethics literature has come of age with respect to the competent adult patient's role in his health care. Paediatric ethics is still in its infancy. If this book promotes dialogue on how health care decisions should be made in the paediatric population, then I have attained some degree of success, even if the reader disagrees with the process or substance.

Notes

1. American Academy of Pediatrics, Committee on Bioethics, 'Informed Consent, Parental Permission, and Assent in Pediatric Practice', *Pediatrics*, 95 (February 1995), 314–17.
2. See, for example, J. Blustein, *Parents and Children: The Ethics of the Family* (New York: Oxford University Press, 1982); W. Kymlicka, 'Rethinking the Family', *Philosophy and Public Affairs*, 20 (1991), 77–97;

and S. M. Okin, *Justice, Gender and the Family* (New York: Basic Books, 1989).

3. M. O. Steinfels, 'Children's Rights, Parental Rights, Family Privacy and Family Autonomy', in W. Gaylin and R. Macklin (eds.), *Who Speaks for the Child: The Problems of Proxy Consent* (New York: Plenum Press, 1982), 253.

4. B. Williams, 'Persons, Character, and Morality', in B. Williams, *Moral Luck* (New York: Cambridge University Press, 1988), 18.

5. A. E. Buchanan and D. W. Brock, *Deciding for Others: The Ethics of Surrogate Decision Making* (New York: Cambridge University Press, 1989), 133.

6. I. Kant, *Grounding for the Metaphysics of Morals* (1785), trans. J. W. Ellington (Indianapolis, Ind.: Hackett Publishing, 1981).

7. R. S. Downie and E. Telfer, *Respect for Persons* (New York: Schocken Books, 1970).

Bibliography

Abernethy, V. 'Compassion, Control, and Decisions about Competency', *American Journal of Psychiatry*, 141 (1984), 113–25.

Abramovitch, R., Freedman, J. L., Thoden, K., and Nikolich, C. 'Children's Capacity to Consent to Participation in Psychological Research: Empirical Findings', *Child Development*, 62 (1991), 1100–9.

Ackerman, T. F. 'Moral Duties of Investigators Toward Sick Children', *IRB: A Review of Human Subjects Research*, 3 (June/July 1981), 1–5.

—— 'Fooling Ourselves with Child Autonomy and Assent in Non-therapeutic Clinical Research', *Clinical Research*, 27 (December 1979), 345–8.

Aiken, W., and LaFollette, H. (eds.). *Whose Child? Children's Rights, Parental Authority and State Power.* Totowa, NJ: Littlefield, Adams, 1980.

Alderson, P. *Children's Consent to Surgery.* Buckingham: Open University Press, 1993.

—— *Choosing for Children: Parents' Consent to Surgery.* Oxford: Oxford University Press, 1990.

—— 'Everyday and Medical Life Choices: Decision-Making Among 8- to 15-Year-Old School Students', *Child: Care, Health and Development*, 18 (1992): 81–95.

Alderson, P., and Montgomery, J. *Health Care Choices: Making Decisions with Children.* London: Institute for Public Policy Research, 1996.

Alonso, E. M., et al. '"Split-Liver" Orthotopic Liver Transplantation (OLT)', *Pediatric Research*, 25 (1989), 107A, Abstract.

American Academy of Pediatrics, Committee on Adolescence. 'Contraception and Adolescents', *Pediatrics*, 86 (1990), 134–8.

American Academy of Pediatrics, Committee on Bioethics. 'Informed Consent, Parental Permission, and Assent in Pediatric Practice', *Pediatrics*, 95 (1995), 314–17.

American Medical Association, Council on Long Range Planning and Development. *AMA Policy Compendium.* Chicago, Ill.: AMA, 1990.

American Medical Association, Council on Scientific Affairs. 'Adolescents as Victims of Family Violence', *JAMA*, 270 (1993), 1850–6.

—— 'Council Report: Confidential Health Services for Adolescents', *JAMA*, 269 (1993), 1420–4.

Appelbaum, P. S., Lidz, C. W., and Meisel, A. *Informed Consent: Legal Theory and Clinical Practice.* New York: Oxford University Press, 1987.

Archard, D. 'Child Abuse: Parental Rights and the Interests of the Child', *Journal of Applied Philosophy*, 7 (1990), 183–94.

—— *Children: Rights and Childhood*. New York: Routledge, 1993.

Aristotle. *The Works of Aristotle*, trans. under the editorship of W. D. Ross, by arrangement with Oxford University Press. Chicago, Ill.: Encyclopaedia Britannica, 1952.

Badhwar, N. K. (ed.). *Friendship: A Philosophical Reader*. Ithaca, NY: Cornell University Press, 1993.

Baker, M. T., and Taub, H. A. 'Readability of Informed Consent Forms for Research in a Veterans Administration Medical Center', *JAMA*, 250 (1983), 2646–8.

Bartholome, W. G. 'Parents, Children, and the Moral Benefits of Research', *Hastings Center Report*, 6 (1976), 44–5.

Baskin, S. 'State Intrusion into Family Affairs: Justifications and Limitations', *Stanford Law Review*, 26 (1974), 1383–1409.

Beauchamp, T. L., and Childress, J. F. *Principles of Biomedical Ethics*, 3rd ed. New York: Oxford University Press, 1989.

Beecher, H. K. 'Ethics and Clinical Research', *New England Journal of Medicine*, 274 (1966), 1354–60.

—— *Research and the Individual*. Boston, Mass.: Little, Brown, 1970.

Bellotti v. Baird, 332 U.S. 622 (1979).

Bismuth H., and Houssin D. 'Reduced-Sized Orthotopic Liver Graft in Hepatic Transplantation in Children', *Surgery*, 95 (1984), 367–70.

Blum, L. *Friendship, Altruism and Morality*. Boston, Mass.: Routledge and Kegan Paul, 1980.

Blustein, J. 'On Children and Proxy Consent', *Journal of Medical Ethics*, 4 (1978), 138–40.

—— 'On the Doctrine of *Parens Patriae*: Fiduciary Obligations and State Power', *Criminal Justice Ethics*, 2 (1983), 39–46.

—— 'On the Duties of Parents and Children', *Southern Journal of Philosophy*, 15 (1977), 427–41.

—— *Parents and Children: The Ethics of the Family*. New York: Oxford University Press, 1982.

—— 'Parents, Paternalism and Children's Rights', *Journal of Critical Analysis*, 8 (1980), 89–98.

Bridges, D. 'Non-paternalistic Arguments in Support of Parents' Rights', *Journal of Philosophy of Education*, 18 (1984), 55–61.

British Paediatric Association. *Guidelines for the Ethical Conduct of Medical Research Involving Children*. London: BPA, 1992.

—— 'Guidelines to Aid Ethical Committees Considering Research Involving Children', *Archives of Diseases of Childhood*, 55 (1980), 75–7.

Brody, B. *Life and Death Decision Making*. New York: Oxford University Press, 1988.

Brody, H. *The Healer's Power*. New Haven, Conn.: Yale University Press, 1992.

Broelsch C. E., et al. 'Liver Transplantation Including the Concept of Reduced-Size Liver Transplants in Children', *Annals of Surgery*, 208 (1988), 410–20.

Brown, D. (ed.). *Risk and Outcome in Anesthesia*, 2nd ed. Philadelphia, Pa.: J. B. Lipincott, 1992.

Buchanan, A. E., and Brock, D. W. *Deciding for Others: The Ethics of Surrogate Decision Making*. New York: Cambridge University Press, 1989.

Cagampang, H. H., Barth, R. P., Korpi, M., and Kirby, D. 'Education Now and Babies Later (ENABL): Life History of a Campaign to Postpone Sexual Involvement', *Family Planning Perspectives*, 19 (1997), 109–14.

Caplan, A. L., Blank, R. H., and Merrick, J. C. *Compelled Compassion: Government Intervention in the Treatment of Critically Ill Newborns*. Totowa, NJ: Humana Press, 1992.

Carey v. Population Service International, 431 U.S. 678 (1977).

Cheng, T. L., Savageau, J. A., Sattler, A. L., and DeWitt, T. G. 'Confidentiality in Health Care: A Survey of Knowledge, Perceptions and Attitudes Among High School Students', *JAMA*, 269 (1993), 1404–7.

Child Abuse Amendments of 1984, 42 U.S.C.A. §§ 5101–05, 5111–13, 5115, (1982 and Supp. 1987), 45 C.F.R. § 1340 (1989).

Cohen, H. *Equal Rights for Children*. Totowa, NJ: Littlefield, Adams, 1980.

Coles, R. *The Moral Life of Children*. Boston, Mass.: Houghton Mifflin, 1986.

Conseur, A., Rivara, F. P., Barnoski, R., and Emanuel, I. 'Maternal and Perinatal Risk Factors for Later Delinquency', *Pediatrics*, 99 (1997), 785–90.

Cromer, B. A., and Brown, R. T. 'Update on Pregnancy, Condom Use, and Prevalence of Selected Sexually Transmitted Diseases in Adolescents', *Current Opinion in Obstetrics and Gynecology*, 4 (1992), 855–9.

Curran, W. J., and Beecher, H. K. 'Experimentation in Children: A Reexamination of Legal Ethical Principles', *JAMA*, 210 (1969), 77–83.

Custody of a minor, 1978 Mass. Adv. Sh. 2002, 379 N.E.2d 1053 (1978), *rev'd and aff'd*, 1979 Mass. Adv. Sh. 2124, 393 N.E.2d 836 (1979).

Department of Health and Human Services. (45 C.F.R. Part 46), 'Additional Protections for Children Involved as Subjects in Research', *Federal Register*, 48 (46) (March 8, 1983), 9814–20.

Department of Health and Social Security (DHSS), *Supervision of the Ethics of Clinical Research Investigations and Fetal Research*, HSC(IS) 153. London: DHHS, 1975.

Department of Health, Education and Welfare. (45 C.F.R. Part 46), 'Protection of Human Subjects: Proposed Regulations on Research

Involving Children', *Federal Register*, 43 (141) (July 21, 1978), 31,786–94.

Doe v. Irwin, 428 F. Supp. 1198 (W.D. Mich. 1977).

Doe v. Irwin, 441 F. Supp. 1247 (W.D. Mich. 1977), *rev'd* 615 F.2d 1162 (6th Cir. 1980), *cert. denied*, 449 U.S. 829 (1980).

Donaldson, T. 'Morally Privileged Relationships', *Journal of Value Inquiry*, 24 (1990), 1–15.

Dornbusch, S. M., and Strober, M. H. (eds.). *Feminism: Children and the New Families*. New York: Guilford Press, 1988.

Dorr, R. T., and Paxinos, J. 'The Current Status of Laetrile', *Annals of Internal Medicine*, 89 (1978), 389–97.

Downie, R. S., and Calman, K. C. *Healthy Respect: Ethics in Health Care*, 2nd ed. New York: Oxford University Press, 1994.

Downie, R. S., and Telfer, E. *Respect for Persons*. New York: Schocken Books, 1970.

Dunn, J. F., et al. 'Living Related Kidney Donors: A 14-Year Experience', *Annals of Surgery*, 203 (1986), 637–42.

Durbin, M., DiClemente, R. J., Siegel, D., Krasnovsky, F., Lazarus, N., and Camacho, T. 'Factors Associated with Multiple Sex Partners Among Junior High School Students', *Journal of Adolescent Health*, 14 (1993), 202–7.

Elshtain, J. B., ed. *The Family in Political Thought*. Amherst, Mass.: University of Massachusetts Press, 1982.

Elster, J. *Solomonic Judgements: Studies in the Limitation of Rationality*. New York: Cambridge University Press, 1989.

Emans, S. J. H., and Goldstein, D. P. *Pediatric and Adolescent Gynecology*, 3rd ed. Boston Mass.: Little, Brown, 1990.

Engelhardt, H. T., Jr. *The Foundations of Bioethics*. New York: Oxford University Press, 1986.

Erikson, E. *Childhood and Society*, 35th anniversary ed. New York: W.W. Norton, 1985.

Estey, E., et al. 'Therapeutic Response in Phase I Trials of Antineoplastic Agents', *Cancer Treatment Reports*, 70 (1986), 1105–15.

Faber-Langendoen, K. 'Resuscitation of Patients with Metastatic Cancer: Is Transient Benefit Still Futile?', *Archives of Internal Medicine*, 151 (1991), 235–9.

Faden, R. R., and Beauchamp, T. L. *A History and Theory of Informed Consent*. New York: Oxford University Press, 1986.

Feinberg, J. *The Moral Limits of the Criminal Law*, i: *Harm to Others*. New York: Oxford University Press, 1984.

—— *The Moral Limits of the Criminal Law*, ii: *Offense to Others*. New York: Oxford University Press, 1985.

Feinberg, J., and Gross, H. (eds.). *Justice: Selected Readings*. Belmont, Calif.: Dickenson Publishing, 1977.

Fellner, C., and Marshall, J. 'Kidney Donors: The Myth of Informed Consent', *American Journal of Psychiatry*, 126 (1970), 1247–51.

Fern, R. L. 'Adolescent Sexuality and the L-Word: How Liberal a Liberalism?', *Politics and the Life Sciences*, 15 (September 1996), 290–2.

Fishkin, J. S. *Justice, Equal Opportunity, and the Family*. New Haven, Conn.: Yale University Press, 1983.

Foster v. Harrison, Eq. No. 68674 (Mass., November 20, 1957).

Freedman, B. 'Equipoise and the Ethics of Clinical Research', *New England Journal of Medicine*, 317 (1987), 141–5.

Freund, P. A. (ed.). *Experimentation with Human Subjects*. New York: George Braziller, 1970.

Friedman, M. *What Are Friends For? Feminist Perspectives on Personal Relationships and Moral Theory*. Ithaca, NY: Cornell University Press, 1993.

Furman, W. L., et al. 'Mortality in Pediatric Phase I Clinical Trials', *Journal of the National Cancer Institute*, 81 (1989), 1193–4.

Galston, W. *Liberal Purposes: Goods, Virtues, and Diversity in the Liberal State*. New York: Cambridge University Press, 1991.

Gardner, W., Scherer, D., and Tester, M. 'Asserting Scientific Authority: Cognitive Development and Adolescent Legal Rights', *American Psychologist*, 44 (1989), 897–9.

Gaylin, W., and Macklin, R. (eds.). *Who Speaks for the Child?: The Problems of Proxy Consent*. New York: Plenum Press, 1982.

German Reich. 'Circular of the Ministry of the Interior on Directives Concerning New Medical Treatments and Scientific Experiments on Man' (1931), trans. in *International Digest of Health Legislation* (Geneva), 31 (1980), 408–11.

Gilligan, C. *In A Different Voice: Psychological Theory and Women's Development*. Cambridge, Mass.: Harvard University Press, 1982.

Gilligan, C., Lyons, N. P., and Hanmer, T. J. (eds.). *Making Connections: The Relational Worlds of Adolescent Girls at Emma Willard School*. Cambridge, Mass.: Harvard University Press, 1990.

Gillick v. W Norfolk & Wisbech HA [1985] 3 All ER 402.

Goldstein, J., Freud, A., and Solnit, A. J. *Before the Best Interests of the Child*, ii. New York: Free Press, 1979.

—— *Beyond the Best Interests of the Child*, i, rev. ed. New York: Free Press, 1979.

Goldstein, J., Freud, A., Solnit, A., and Goldstein, S. *In the Best Interest of the Child*, iii. New York: Free Press, 1986.

182 *Bibliography*

Goodin, R. E. *Protecting the Vulnerable: A Reanalysis of our Social Responsibilities*. Chicago, Ill.: University of Chicago Press, 1985.

Goodman, M. F. *What Is a Person?* Clifton, NJ: Humana Press, 1988.

Graham, G., and LaFollette, H. (eds.). *Person to Person*. Philadelphia, Pa.: Temple University Press, 1989.

Graham, K. (ed.). *Contemporary Political Philosophy: Radical Studies*. New York: Cambridge University Press, 1982.

Green, O. H. (ed.). *Respect for Persons*, Tulane Studies in Philosophy 31. New Orleans, La.: Tulane University Press, 1982.

Grisso, T., and Vierling, L. 'Minors' Consent to Treatment: A Developmental Perspective', *Professional Psychology*, 9 (1978), 412–27.

Griswold v. Connecticut, 381 U.S. 479, 85 S. Ct. 1678, 14 L. Ed.2d 510 (1965).

Grodin, M. A., and Glantz, L. H. (eds.). *Children as Research Subjects: Science, Ethics, and Law*. New York: Oxford University Press, 1994.

Grubb, A. (ed.). *Choices and Decisions in Health Care*. New York: John Wiley and Sons, 1993.

Grunder, T. M. 'On the Readability of Surgical Consent Forms', *New England Journal of Medicine*, 302 (1980), 900–2.

Guetzkow, H. (ed.), for the U.S. Office of Naval Research. *Groups, Leadership and Men: Research in Human Relations*. Pittsburgh, Pa.: Carnegie Press, 1951.

Gutmann, A. 'Children, Paternalism and Education: A Liberal Argument', *Philosophy and Public Affairs*, 9 (1980), 338–58.

Hakim, R. M., Goldszer, R. C., and Brenner, B. M. 'Hypertension and Proteinuria: Long-Term Sequelae of Uninephrectomy in Humans', *Kidney International*, 25 (1984), 930–6.

Hardwig, J. 'Should Women Think in Terms of Rights?', *Ethics*, 94 (1984), 441–55.

Hart v. Brown, 29 Conn. Supp. 368, 289 A.2d 386 (Super. Ct. 1972).

Harth, S. C., Johnstone, R. R., and Thong, Y. H. 'The Psychological Profile of Parents Who Volunteer Their Children for Clinical Research: A Controlled Study', *Journal of Medical Ethics*, 18 (1992), 86–93.

Hattab, J. Y. (ed.). *Ethics and Child Mental Health*. Jerusalem: Gefen Publishing House, 1994.

Hegel, G. W. F. *Philosophy of Right* (1821), trans. with notes by T. M. Knox. New York: Oxford University Press, 1967.

Hendry, L. B., Roberts, W., Glendinning, A., and Coleman, J. C. 'Adolescents' Perception of Significant Individuals in Their Lives', *Journal of Adolescence*, 15 (1992), 255–70.

Hill, T. E., Jr. *Autonomy and Self-Respect*. New York: Cambridge University Press, 1991.

Hirshberg, B. A. 'Who Speaks for the Child and What Are His Rights?: A

Proposed Standard for Evaluation', *Law and Human Behavior*, 4 (1980), 217–36.

Hirschman, A. O. *Exit, Voice and Loyalty: Responses to Decline in Firms, Organizations and States*. Cambridge, Mass.: Harvard University Press, 1970.

Hobbes, T. *De Corpore Politico* (1640). In R. S. Peter (ed.), *Body, Man and Citizen*. New York: Collier Press, 1967.

—— 'Philosophical Rudiments Concerning Government and Society'. In W. Molesworth (ed.), *The English Works of Thomas Hobbes*, ii. London: John Bohn, 1966.

Hobson, P. 'Some Reflections on Parents' Rights in the Upbringing of Their Children', *Journal of Philosophy of Education*, 18 (1984), 63–74.

Holder, A. *Legal Issues in Pediatrics and Adolescent Medicine*, 2nd ed. New Haven, Conn.: Yale University Press, 1985.

Holland, J. C. 'Patients Who Seek Unproven Cancer Remedies: A Psychological Perspective', *Clinical Bulletin*, 11 (1981), 102–5.

Holt, J. *Escape from Childhood*. New York: E. P. Dutton, 1974.

Houlgate, L. *Family and State: The Philosophy of Family Law*. Totowa, NJ: Rowman and Littlefield, 1988.

—— *The Child and the State: A Normative Theory of Juvenile Rights*. Baltimore, Md.: Johns Hopkins University Press, 1980.

Humm, S. R., Ort, B. A., Anbari, M. M., Lader, W. S., and Biel, W. S. (eds.). *Child, Parent, and State*. Philadelphia, Pa.: Temple University Press, 1994.

Huskey v. Harrison, Eq. No. 68666 (Mass., August 30, 1957).

In re Carson, 39 Misc.2d 544, 545, 241 N.Y.S.2d 288, 289 (1962).

In re Green, 448 Pa. 338, 292 A.2d 387 (1972).

In re Hofbauer, 65 A.D.2d 108, 411 N.Y.S.2d 416 (1978), *aff'd* 47 N.Y.2d 1009, 419 N.Y.S.2d 936 (1979).

In re Richardson, 284 So.2d 185 La. App. (1973).

In re Sampson, 65 Misc.2d 658, 317 N.Y.S.2d 641 (Fam. Ct. 1970) *aff'd*, 37 App. Div.2d 668, 323 N.Y.S.2d 253 (1971), *aff'd*, 29 N.Y.2d 900, 278 N.E.2d 918, 328 N.Y.S.2d 686 (1972).

In re Seiferth, 309 N.Y. 80; 127 N.E.2d 820 (1955).

Inness, J. *Privacy, Intimacy, and Isolation*. New York: Oxford University Press, 1992.

Jacobson v. Massachusetts, 197 U.S. 11 (1905).

James, A., and Prout, A. (eds). *Constructing and Reconstructing Childhood: New Directions in the Sociological Study of Childhood*. Basingstoke: Falmer Press, 1990.

Janofsky, J., and Starfield, B. 'Assessment of Risk in Research on Children', *Journal of Pediatrics*, 98 (1981), 842–6.

Johnson, N., Lilford, R. J., and Brazier, W. 'At What Level of Collective

Equipoise Does a Clinical Trial Become Ethical?', *Journal of Medical Ethics*, 17 (1991), 30–4.

Jonsen, A. R., Siegler, M., and Winslade, W. J. *Clinical Ethics*, 3rd ed. New York: McGraw-Hill, 1992.

Juszczak, L. 'Adolescent Parenthood'. In S. B. Friedman, M. Fisher, and S. K. Schonberg (eds.), *Comprehensive Adolescent Health Care*. St Louis, Mo.: Quality Medical Publishing, 1992.

Kant, I. *Grounding for the Metaphysics of Morals* (1785), trans. J. W. Ellington. Indianapolis, Ind.: Hackett Publishing, 1981.

Katz, J. *The Silent World of Doctor and Patient*. New York: Free Press, 1984.

—— 'Why Doctors Don't Disclose Uncertainty', *Hastings Center Report*, 14 (1984), 35–44.

Kempe, C. H., Silver, H. K., and O'Brien, D. *Current Pediatric Diagnosis and Treatment*, 7th ed. Los Altos, Calif.: Lange Medical Publications, 1982.

Kittay, E. F., and Meyers, D. T. (eds.). *Women and Moral Theory*. Savage, Md.: Rowman and Littlefield, 1987.

Kliever, L. D. (ed.). *Dax's Case: Essays in Medical Ethics and Human Meaning*. Dallas, Tex.: Southern Methodist University Press, 1988.

Ku, L. C., Sonenstein, F. C., and Pleck, J. H. 'The Association of AIDS Education and Sex Education with Sexual Behavior and Condom Use Among Teenage Men', *Family Planning Perspectives*, 24 (1992), 100–6.

Kymlicka, W. *Liberalism, Community and Culture*. New York: Oxford University Press, 1989.

—— 'Rethinking the Family'. *Philosophy and Public Affairs*, 20 (1991), 77–97.

Ladd, J., 'The Idea of Community', *New England Journal* (occasional publication of the New England Chapter of the American Institute of Planners), 1 (1972), 1–43.

Ladd, R. E. *Children's Rights Re-Visioned: Philosophical Readings*. Belmont, Calif.: Wadsworth Publishing, 1996.

——— (ed.). 'Paternalism and the Rationality of the Child', *Thinking: The Journal of Philosophy for Children*, 6 (1984), 15–19.

LaFollette, H. *Personal Relationships: Love, Identity, and Morality*. Cambridge, Mass.: Blackwell Publishers, 1996.

Lantos, J. D., et al. 'The Illusion of Futility in Clinical Practice', *American Journal of Medicine*, 87 (1989), 81–4.

Lascari, A. 'Risks of Research in Children', *Journal of Pediatrics*, 98 (1981), 759–60.

Lasch, C. *Haven in a Heartless World: The Family Besieged*. New York: Basic Books, 1977.

Leiken, S. L. 'An Ethical Issue in Biomedical Research: The Involvement of Minors in Informed and Third Party Consent', *Clinical Research*, 31 (1983), 34–40.

Levine, R. J. *Ethics and Regulation of Clinical Research,* 2nd ed. New Haven, Conn.: Yale University Press, 1988.

Locke, J. *Two Treatises of Government* (1690), rev. ed., ed. with intro. and apparatus criticus by P. Laslett. New York: New American Library, 1963.

Lockhart, J. D. 'Pediatric Drug Testing? Is It at Risk?' *Hastings Center Report,* 7 (1977), 8–10.

Lomasky, L. E. *Persons, Rights and the Moral Community.* New York: Oxford University Press, 1987.

Lynskey, M. 'Universal Solutions or Individual Choices', *Politics and the Life Sciences,* 15 (1996), 295–6.

Mahowald, M. B. *Women and Children in Health Care: An Unequal Majority.* New York: Oxford University Press, 1993.

Masden v. Harrison, Eq. No. 68651 (Mass., June 12, 1957).

McCormick, R. A. 'Experimentation in Children: Sharing in Sociality', *Hastings Center Report,* 6 (1976), 41–6.

—— 'Proxy Consent in the Experimentation Situation', *Perspectives in Biology and Medicine,* 18 (1974), 2–23.

Medical Research Council. 'Responsibility in Investigations on Human Subjects', *Report of the Medical Research Council for the Year 1962–63.* London: Her Majesty's Stationery Office, 1964.

Medical Research Council, Working Party on Research on Children. *The Ethical Conduct of Research on Children.* London: MRC, 1991.

Meyer v. Nebraska, 262 U.S. 390 (1923).

Meyers, D., Kipnis, K., and Murphy, C. F., Jr. (eds.). *Kindred Matters: Rethinking the Philosophy of the Family.* Ithaca, NY: Cornell University Press, 1993.

Milgram, S. *Obedience to Authority: An Experimental View.* New York: Harper and Row, 1974.

Minow, M. 'Redefining Families: Who's In and Who's Out?', *University of Colorado Law Review,* 62 (1991), 269–85.

—— 'Rights for the Next Generation: A Feminist Approach to Children's Rights', *Harvard Women's Law Journal,* 9 (1986), 1–24.

Mintz, S., and Kellogg, S. *Domestic Revolutions: A Social History of American Family Life.* New York: Free Press, 1988.

Mnookin, R. H., and Weisberg, D. K. (eds.). *Child, Family and State: Problems and Materials on Children and the Law,* 2nd ed. Boston, Mass.: Little, Brown, 1989.

Morbidity and Mortality Weekly Report. 'Sexual Behavior Among High School Students—United States, 1990', *MMWR—Morbidity and Mortality Weekly Report,* 40 (1992), 885–8.

Moertel, C. G., et al. 'A Clinical Trial of Amygdalin (Laetrile) in the

Treatment of Human Cancer', *New England Journal of Medicine*, 306 (1982), 201–6.

Najarian, J. S., Chavers, B. M., McHugh, L. E., and Matas, A. J. '20 Years or More of Follow-Up of Living Kidney Donors', *Lancet*, 340 (8823) (1992), 807–10.

Nathan v. Farinelli, Eq. No. 74–87 (Mass., July 3, 1974).

National Center for Health Statistics. 'Advance Report of Final Natality Statistics, 1990', *Monthly Vital Statistics Report*, 41 Supp. (1993).

National Commission for the Protection of Human Subjects. *Report and Recommendations: Research Involving Children*. Washington, DC: U.S. Printing Office, 1977.

Navarro, M. 'Teen-Age Mothers Viewed as Abused Prey of Older Men', *New York Times*, 19 May 1996, 1 and 11.

Nelson, J. L. 'Partialism and Parenthood', *Journal of Social Philosophy*, 21 (1990), 107–8.

Nicholson, L. *Gender and History: The Limits of Social Theory in the Age of the Family*. New York: Columbia University Press, 1986.

Nicholson, R. H. (ed.). *Medical Research with Children: Ethics, Law, and Practice*. Oxford: Oxford University Press, 1986.

Noller, P., and Fitzpatrick, M. A. *Communication in Family Relationships*. Englewood Cliffs, NJ: Prentice Hall, 1993.

Okin, S. M. *Justice, Gender and the Family*. New York: Basic Books, 1989.

—— 'Women and the Making of the Sentimental Family', *Philosophy and Public Affairs*, 11 (1982), 65–88.

—— *Women in Western Political Thought*. Princeton, NJ: Princeton University Press, 1979.

O'Neill, O. 'Children's Rights and Children's Lives', *Ethics*, 98 (1988), 445–63.

O'Neill, O., and Ruddick, W. (eds.). *Having Children: Philosophical and Legal Reflections on Parenthood*. Oxford: Oxford University Press, 1979.

Page, E. 'Parental Rights', *Journal of Applied Philosophy*, 1 (1984), 187–203.

Paris, J. J., Crone, R. K., and Reardon, F. 'Physicians' Refusal of Requested Treatment: The Case of Baby L', *New England Journal of Medicine*, 322 (1990), 1012–13.

Pellegrino, E. D., and Thomasma, D. C. *For the Patient's Good: The Restoration of Beneficence in Health Care*. New York: Oxford University Press, 1988.

Pendergrass, T. W., and Davis, S. 'Knowledge and Use of Alternative Cancer Therapies in Children', *American Journal of Pediatric Hematology-Oncology*, 3 (1981), 339–445.

Perrin, E., and Gerrity, P. S. 'There's a Demon in Your Belly: Children's Understanding of Illness', *Pediatrics*, 67 (1981), 841–9.

Perry, J., and Bratman, M. (eds.). *Introduction of Philosophy: Classical and*

Contemporary Readings, 2nd ed. New York: Oxford University Press, 1993.

Phillips, D. *Toward a Just Social Order*. Princeton, NJ: Princeton University Press, 1986.

Piaget, J. *The Child's Conception of Physical Causality*. Patterson, NJ: Littlefield, Adams, 1960.

—— *The Moral Judgment of the Child*, trans. M. Gabain. New York: Free Press, 1965.

Pierce v. Society of Sisters, 268 U.S. 510 (1925).

Planned Parenthood of Central Missouri v. Danforth, 428 U.S. 52 (1976).

President's Commission for the Study of Ethical Problems in Medicine and Biomedical and Behavioral Research. *Making Health Care Decisions: The Ethical and Legal Implications of Informed Consent in the Patient-Practitioner Relationship*, i. Washington, DC: U.S. Government Printing Office, 1982.

Price, J. H., and Price, J. A. 'Laetrile–An Overview', *Journal of School Health*, 48 (1978), 409–16.

Pui, C.-H. 'Acute Lymphoblastic Leukemia', *Pediatric Clinics of North America*, 44 (1997), 831–46.

Purdy, L. *In Their Best Interest: The Case Against Equal Rights for Children*. Ithaca, NY: Cornell University Press, 1992.

Ramsey, P. 'Children as Research Subjects: A Reply', *Hastings Center Report*, 7 (1977), 40–1.

—— 'The Enforcement of Morals: Nontherapeutic Research on Children', *Hastings Center Report*, 6 (1976), 21–30.

—— *The Patient as Person: Explorations in Medical Ethics*. New Haven, Conn.: Yale University Press, 1970.

Rawls, J. *A Theory of Justice*. Cambridge, Mass.: Belknap Press of Harvard University Press, 1971.

—— *Political Liberalism*. New York: Columbia University Press, 1993.

Re E [1993] 1 FLR 386.

Re R [1991] 4 All ER 177.

Re S (1994) 2 FLR 1065.

Re W [1992] 4 All ER 627.

Reich, W. T. (ed.-in-chief). *Encyclopedia of Bioethics*. New York: Free Press, 1978.

Robertson, J. A. *Children of Choice: Freedom and the New Reproductive Technologies*. Princeton, NJ: Princeton University Press, 1994.

Rodham, H. 'Children's Rights: A Legal Perspective.' In P. A. Vardin and I. N. Brody (eds.), *Children's Rights: Contemporary Perspectives*. New York: Teachers College Press, 1979.

—— 'Children Under the Law', *Harvard Educational Review*, 43 (1973), 487–514.

Roe v. Wade, 410 U.S. 113 (1973).

Ross, J. J. *The Virtues of the Family*. New York: Free Press, 1994.

Royal College of Physicians, *Supervision of the Ethics of Clinical Research Investigations in Institutions*. London: Royal College of Physicians, 1973.

Salgo v Leland Stanford Jr. University Board of Trustees, 317 P 2d 170 (Cal. Dist. Ct. App., 1957).

Sandel, M. *Liberalism and the Limits of Justice*. New York: Cambridge University Press, 1982.

Scarre, G. 'Children and Paternalism', *Philosophy*, 55 (1980), 117–24.

—— (ed.). *Children, Parents and Politics*. New York: Cambridge University Press, 1989.

Scherer, D. G., and Reppucci, N. D. 'Adolescents' Capacities to Provide Voluntary Informed Consent: The Effects of Parental Influence and Medical Dilemmas', *Law and Human Behavior*, 12 (1988), 123–41.

Schneiderman, L., Jecker, N., and Jonsen, A. 'Medical Futility: Its Meaning and Ethical Implications', *Annals of Internal Medicine*, 112 (1990), 949–54.

Schoeman, F. 'Book Review: *Family and State: The Philosophy of Family Law*, by Laurence Houlgate', *Ethics*, 99 (1989), 651–5.

—— 'Childhood Competence and Autonomy', *Journal of Legal Studies*, 12 (1983), 267–87.

—— 'Parental Discretion and Children's Rights: Background and Implications for Medical Decision-Making', *Journal of Medicine and Philosophy*, 10 (1985), 45–62.

—— 'Rights of Children, Rights of Parents, and the Moral Basis of the Family', *Ethics*, 91 (1980), 6–19.

Schrag, F. 'Justice and the Family', *Inquiry*, 19 (1976), 193–208.

—— 'Rights over Children', *Journal of Value Inquiry*, 8 (1973), 96–105.

—— 'The Child in the Moral Order', *Philosophy*, 52 (1977), 167–77.

Schultz, A. L., Pardee, G. P., and Ensinck, J. W. 'Are Research Subjects Really Informed?' *Western Journal of Medicine*, 123 (1975), 76–80.

Schwartz, A. H. 'Children's Concepts of Research Hospitalization', *New England Journal of Medicine*, 287 (1972), 589–92.

Sher, E. 'Choosing for Children: Adjudicating Medical Care Disputes Between Parents and the State', *New York University Law Review*, 58 (1983), 157–206.

Shimp v. McFall, 10 Pa. D. & C.3d 90 (C.P. Ct. 1978).

Shope, J. T. 'Medication Compliance', *Pediatric Clinics of North America*, 28 (1981), 5–21.

Sigman, G. S., and O'Connor, C. 'Exploration for Physicians of the Mature Minor Doctrine', *Journal of Pediatrics*, 119 (1991), 520–5.

Silverman, W. A. 'The Myth of Informed Consent in Daily Practice and in Clinical Trials', *Journal of Medical Ethics*, 15 (1989), 6–11.

Sokolosky, W. 'The Sick Child and the Reluctant Parent—A Framework for Judicial Intervention', *Journal of Family Law*, 20 (1981–2), 69–104.

Somerville, C. J. *The Rise and Fall of Childhood*, rev. ed. New York: Vintage Books, 1990.

Spitz, A. M., et al. 'Pregnancy, Abortion and Birth Rates among U.S. Adolescents—1980, 1985, and 1990', *JAMA*, 275 (1996), 989–94.

Stephenson, B. J., et al. 'Is This Patient Taking the Treatment as Prescribed?', *JAMA*, 269 (1993), 2779–81.

Sunstein, C. (ed.). *Feminism and Political Theory*. Chicago, Ill.: University of Chicago Press, 1990.

Superintendent of Belchertown State School v. Saikewicz, 373 Mass. 728, 370 N.E.2d 417 (1977).

Susman, E. J., Dorn, L. D., and Fletcher, J. C. 'Reasoning About Illness in Ill and Healthy Children and Adolescents: Cognitive and Emotional Developmental Aspects', *Developmental and Behavioral Pediatrics*, 8 (1987), 266–73.

Tarnowski, K. J., Allen, D. M., Mayhall, C., and Kelly, P. A. 'Readability of Pediatric Biomedical Research Informed Consent Forms', *Pediatrics*, 85 (1990), 58–62.

Thompson, R. 'Vulnerability in Research: A Developmental Perspective on Research Risk', *Child Development*, 61 (1990), 1–16.

Thorne, B. (ed.), with Yalom, M. *Rethinking the Family: Some Feminist Questions*, rev. ed. Boston, Mass.: Northeastern University Press, 1992.

Tomlinson, T., and Brody, H. 'Futility and the Ethics of Resuscitation', *JAMA*, 264 (1990), 1276–80.

Tönnies, F. *Gemeinschaft und Gesellschaft*, trans. C. P. Loomis as *Community and Society*. East Lansing, Mich.: Michigan State University Press, 1957.

Truog, R. D., Brett, A. S., and Frader, J. 'The Problem with Futility', *New England Journal of Medicine*, 326 (1992), 1560–4.

U.S. Congress, Office of Technology Assessment. *Adolescent Health: Volume I—Background and the Effectiveness of Selected Prevention and Treatment Service*. Washington, DC: U.S. Government Printing Office, 1992.

Vardin, P. A., and Brody, I. N. (eds.). *Children's Rights: Contemporary Perspectives*. New York: Teachers College Press, 1979.

Veatch, R. M. *Patient-Physician Relation: Patient as Partner*, Part II. Bloomington, Ind.: Indiana University Press, 1991.

—— *The Foundations of Justice: Why the Retarded and the Rest of Us Have Claims to Equality*. New York: Oxford University Press, 1986.

Waldron, J. 'When Justice Replaces Affection: The Need for Rights', *Harvard Journal of Law and Public Policy*, 11 (1988), 625–47.

Walzer, M. *Spheres of Justice: A Defense of Pluralism and Equality*. New York: Basic Books, 1983.

Wardle, L. 'Parents' Rights vs. Minors' Rights Regarding the Provision of Contraceptives to Teenagers', *Nebraska Law Review*, 68 (1989), 216–60.

Weir, R. F., and Peters, C. 'Affirming the Decisions Adolescents Make About Life and Death, *Hastings Center Report*, 27 (1997), 29–40.

Weithorn, L., and Campbell, S. 'The Competency of Children and Adolescents to Make Informed Treatment Decisions', *Child Development*, 53 (1982), 1589–98.

White, B. C. *Competence to Consent*. Washington, DC: Georgetown University Press, 1994.

Williams, B. *Moral Luck*. New York: Cambridge University Press, 1988.

Williams, P. 'Success in Spite of Failure: Why IRBs Falter in Reviewing Risks and Benefits', *IRB: A Review of Human Subjects Research*, 6 (May/June 1984), 1–4.

Wisconsin v. Yoder, 406 U.S. 205 (1972).

Wolpe, P. R. 'Adolescent Contraception and the Just Society', *Politics and Life Sciences*, 15 (1996), 321–3.

Worthington, E. L., et al. 'Mandatory Parental Involvement Prior to Adolescent Abortion', *Journal of Adolescent Health*, 12 (1991), 138–42.

Young, I. M. 'Rights to Intimacy in a Complex Society', *Journal of Social Philosophy* (1982), 47–52.

Youngner, S. 'Who Defines Futility?' *JAMA*, 260 (1988), 2094–5.

Index